Current Chinese Economic Report Series

AF785962

The Current Chinese Economic Reports series provides insights into the economic development of one of the largest and fastest growing economies in the world; though widely discussed internationally, many facets of its current development remain unknown to the English speaking world. All reports contain new data, which was previously unknown or unavailable outside of China. The series covers regional development, industry reports, as well as special topics like environmental or demographical issues.

More information about this series at http://www.springer.com/series/11028

Center for Macroeconomic Research of Xiamen University

China's Macroeconomic Outlook

Quarterly Forecast and Analysis Report, February 2016

Springer

Center for Macroeconomic Research of Xiamen University
Xiamen, Fujian
China

ISSN 2194-7937 ISSN 2194-7945 (electronic)
Current Chinese Economic Report Series
ISBN 978-981-10-9519-1 ISBN 978-981-10-2068-1 (eBook)
DOI 10.1007/978-981-10-2068-1

© Springer Science+Business Media Singapore 2016
Softcover reprint of the hardcover 1st edition 2016
This work is subject to copyright. All rights are reserved by the Publisher, whether the whole or part of the material is concerned, specifically the rights of translation, reprinting, reuse of illustrations, recitation, broadcasting, reproduction on microfilms or in any other physical way, and transmission or information storage and retrieval, electronic adaptation, computer software, or by similar or dissimilar methodology now known or hereafter developed.
The use of general descriptive names, registered names, trademarks, service marks, etc. in this publication does not imply, even in the absence of a specific statement, that such names are exempt from the relevant protective laws and regulations and therefore free for general use.
The publisher, the authors and the editors are safe to assume that the advice and information in this book are believed to be true and accurate at the date of publication. Neither the publisher nor the authors or the editors give a warranty, express or implied, with respect to the material contained herein or for any errors or omissions that may have been made.

Printed on acid-free paper

This Springer imprint is published by Springer Nature
The registered company is Springer Science+Business Media Singapore Pte Ltd.

Preface

This report is a partial result of the China Quarterly Macroeconomic Model (CQMM), a project of the Center for Macroeconomic Research (CMR) at Xiamen University. The CMR is one of the Key Research Institutes of the Humanities and Social Sciences of the Ministry of Education of China. The research is funded by the Key Project of the National Social Science Fund of China (13&ZD029), the Key Projects of Philosophy and Social Sciences Research of the Ministry of Education of China (15JZD016, 14JZD011), the Major Project for Humanities and Social Sciences Key Research Institutes of the Ministry of Education of China (14JJD790007, 13JJD790026, 13JJD790025), the General and Youth Project of the National Social Science Foundation of China (15BJL008,13CJL017, 11CJY073), and the Youth Project of the National Natural Science Foundation of China (71503222).

Since the launch of CQMM 10 years ago, 19 forecast reports with policy simulations and 10 collections of essays on macroeconomic analyses for China have been published. This is the twentieth forecast report and summarizes the forecast results released at the China Macroeconomic Advanced Forum (Spring 2016) during the CQMM Press Conference for Economic Projections for 2016–2017. The forum was jointly organized by the Center for Macroeconomic Research, Xiamen University, and the Economic Information Daily, Xinhua News Agency, in Beijing on February 25, 2016.

Xiamen, China Center for Macroeconomic Research of Xiamen University

Contents

Contributors

Principal Investigator

Li Wenpu, Center for Macroeconomic Research of Xiamen University, Xiamen, China

Team Members

Wang Yanwu, Li Jing, Gong Min, Lu Shengrong, Wu Huakun, Chen Guifu, Yu Changlin, Miao Xinyue, Zhai Ke, Huo Yao, Li Chenglong, Li Weijie, Shi Danping, Wang Miao

Introduction

In 2015, China's economic growth continued to slow; the real growth rate of China's gross domestic product (GDP) was 6.9 %, 0.4 percentage points lower than that of the previous year and the lowest growth rate over the past 25 years. In the short term, weak demand is the main reason for the current economic slowdown. First, fixed asset investment growth appeared to decline in various industries and for all kinds of investment sources. Second, growth in urban and rural residential real income continued to slow, inhibiting the expansion of residential consumption. Finally, continuing weakness in export demand and a shrinking processing trade industry caused by rising domestic wages inhibited export growth.

In the long run, the economic slowdown is a result of a decline in production efficiency and a structural imbalance between supply and demand caused by the increase of per capita income and demand structure transformation. There is also an imbalance in the structure of income distribution, the slow pace of market-oriented reform in the production factor market, and lagging and imperfect market-oriented reform in financial capital markets. Meanwhile, the economic growth mode has not changed along with the transformation of the economic development stage. These have also become important factors in restricting China's persistent and steady economic growth as its economy moves toward the new normal.

We believe that both supply and demand are needed to solve the problems mentioned above. The problems of total amount and structure cannot be ignored. What's more, while expanding demand, the government should also improve the supply structure and efficiency. If the government pays too much attention to reducing invalid supply and does not expand effective supply, it will not be conducive to steady growth and could lead to a deflation superposition and a downward spiral in the economy. Therefore, according to the demand structure transformation trend caused by the rising per capita income, while removing outdated, excess, and invalid production capacity, the government should also increase new capacity and expand investment and effective supply. This will expand social total demand by expanding investment in effective supply, forming a spiral cycle between social total supply and demand and encouraging innovation to boost growth and stimulating demand to guarantee employment. On the supply side, by reforming the supply structure, the government should not only reduce the invalid supply but also pay more attention to expanding effective supply according to the demand sources and changes in the structure and improve the flexible adaptability of supply efficiency and quality and structure to the demand structure. On the demand side, the government should raise residential income and expand consumer demand by adjusting income distribution. Meanwhile, the government should take full advantage of the role of interest rate liberalization in the efficient allocation of credit resources and ensure that the expanded credit resources fully meet the needs of private investment and promote the adjustment of the industrial structure through effective investment.

The China Quarterly Macroeconomic Model (CQMM) predicts that China's economic growth will continue to fall under the pressure of declining investment over the next 2 years but that the growth reduction will slow. Moreover, the risk of comprehensive deflation is relatively small.

1. We expect that the GDP growth rate will be 6.66 % in 2016, 0.25 percentage points lower than that of 2015. The CPI will rise by 1.48 %, 0.04 percentage points higher than that of 2015. The PPI is expected to be −3.31 %, 1.9 percentage points lower than that of the previous year. The growth rate of the GDP deflator may be 0.09 %, 0.51 percentage points higher than that of 2015.
2. The excess capacity in manufacturing, the excessive inventory of the real estate industry, and corporate debt burdens will continue to put downward pressure on investment. Urban fixed asset investment growth at current prices is expected to be 9.13 % in 2016, 1.11 percentage points lower than that of 2015.
3. In the short term, growth in residential real income is unlikely to increase considerably. Residential consumption habits and propensity are even more unlikely to change greatly. Therefore, residential consumption will continue to maintain its current slow growth over the next 2 years. In 2016, the growth rate of social retail sales at current prices will be 11.53 %, a slight increase of 0.33 percentage points over the previous year.
4. Although the IMF predicts that global trade in goods and services will recover and grow over the next 2 years, the economic growth of major economies remains highly uncertain. China's total exports in USD at current prices are expected to grow by 0.83 %, 3.11 percentage points higher than that of 2015. The growth rate of total imports may fall to −8.36 %, 6.06 percentage points higher than that of 2015.
5. In 2016, there is still a depreciation expectation caused by the economic slowdown and the pressure of capital outflows. China's foreign exchange reserves will continue to shrink to maintain the stability of the RMB exchange rate. Foreign exchange reserves are expected to drop to 3.12 trillion dollars in 2016.

Based on its judgment of China's economic situation over the next 2 years, the research team makes the following policy suggestions:

1. The government should attach great importance to the current economic slowdown, which poses huge risks to China's economy. Due to the economic

slowdown, economic structural adjustments are slowing, and depreciation expectation is entering a self-reinforcing cycle. Economic growth slowdown and intensified structural deflation increase the risk of a debt crisis. The continuous economic slowdown will be seriously detrimental to structural reform on the supply side. Historical experiences at home and abroad have proved that, during structural reform, it is common to reduce supply in some areas while increasing it in others, but this must be based on a certain economic growth.

2. Supply-side structural reform should consider demand structure transformation as a guideline in the context of a new stage of development. While reducing supply in some areas, the government should place emphasis on increasing supply in others, expanding demand, and ensuring its steady growth. China's macroeconomic policy has paid too much attention to the international financial crisis, a cyclical impact from outside, and ignored the structural and institutional adjustments caused by transformation in the new development stage. This led to the current serious excess capacity, insufficient effective supply, and continuous economic slowdown. The government should conduct supply-side reform and reduce supply in some areas while increasing it in others on the basis of the demand structure transformation trend in this new development stage in which an upper-middle-income economy transits to a high-income economy. According to the requirements of the supply-side structure adjustment, expanding investment will not only achieve supply-side structural adjustment faster but will also be conducive to steady growth.
3. The government should take the supply-side structural adjustment as a direction, enlarging investment, fostering steady growth, and adjusting the structure with new capacity. Over the next 10 years, the residential consumption structure will appear in a new round of upgrading transformation with the transition from an upper-middle-income to a high-income economy (China's per capita nominal GDP will exceed $10,000 during the period covered by the 13th Five-Year Plan). At present, residential consumption mainly comprises physical consumption such as housing, transportation, food, and clothing. This will gradually transform into a new consumption structure featuring service consumption and high-quality physical consumption. The proportion of expenditure on education, culture, entertainment, and health care will be significantly improved and become a driving force for consumer demand over the next 10–20 years. In response to the improvement in the consumption structure, the government must change the current situation whereby the effective supply capacity of modern service products is gravely insufficient as soon as possible.
4. The phrase "vacating the cage to change the bird" means that the government should obtain investment funds by investment substitution. The investment growth of the private economy declined in 2015. The loose monetary policy did not allocate credit resources effectively to the real economy, especially the private sector. The limited investment field is another important reason for the slow growth. Therefore, investment substitution will enable government departments to obtain infrastructure investment funds. It will also expand the investment field and increase growth in the private economy at the same time. In

addition, the current state-owned economy is concentrated in the modern service industry. As a result, implementing mixed ownership reform in the related state-owned enterprises will break the monopoly, deregulate, and foster market competition. It will greatly improve the efficiency of resource utilization and production efficiency in the modern service industry and ultimately increase supply efficiency.

5. The value of the RMB should be stabilized to create a good external environment for supply-side structural adjustment. The government should maintain the RMB exchange rate, steadily promote the pace of interest rate liberalization, strengthen the openness and transparency of the policy, and effectively manage market expectations. This will create a good external environment for the domestic supply-side structural adjustment.

Chapter 1
A Review of China's Economy in 2015

In 2015, China's real GDP grew by 6.9 %, a decrease of 0.4 percentage points from the previous year and the lowest of the last 25 years. Influenced by excess production capacity in the upstream manufacturing and a slowdown in export manufacturing, the real growth of industrial added value was 5.9 %, a decrease of 1.0 percentage points from the previous year and the lowest since 1997 (see Fig. 1.1). There were many factors behind the continued decline of China's economy. In demand terms, a continued slowdown of domestic investment demand and a continued slump in international market demand were the main factors. In supply terms, it was the result of structural disequilibrium and productivity impairment due to demand structure transformation. Furthermore, several important constraints impeded the steady and rapid development of China's economy during the "New Normal," such as an imbalance in the income distribution structure, a slowdown of market-oriented reform in the production factor market, a lag and imperfection in market-oriented reform in the capital market, and an inconformity between the economic growth pattern and economic development stages.

1.1 Economic Growth Continued to Fall, and the Economic Structure Adjusted Slowly

China's economy has been adjusting its structure passively and actively since the financial crisis to cope with changes in the economic environment at home and abroad. New space for economic development arose during the conversion of the growth pattern and growth momentum. However, the continued slowdown of the economy meant that structural adjustment could not be promoted in a timely way, which was a problem for current macroeconomic regulation.

© Springer Science+Business Media Singapore 2016

Center for Macroeconomic Research of Xiamen University, *China's Macroeconomic Outlook*, Current Chinese Economic Report Series, DOI 10.1007/978-981-10-2068-1_1

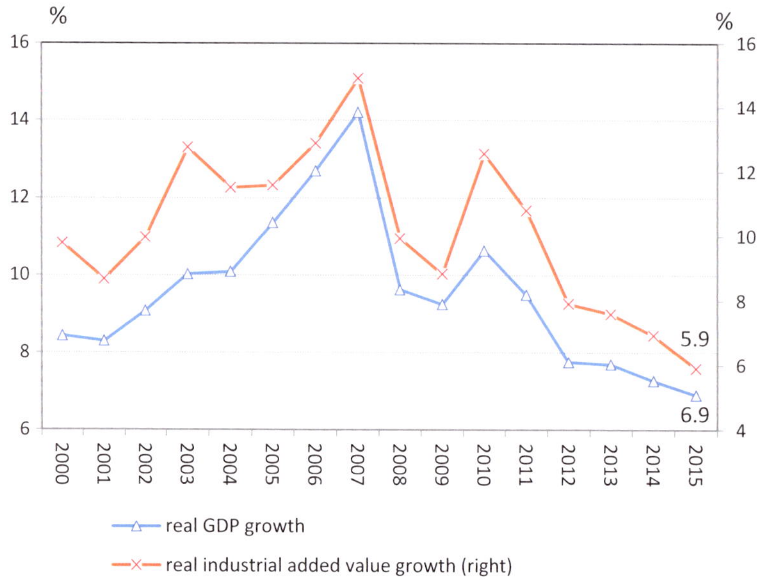

Fig. 1.1 Growth rate changes in China's GDP and industrial added value (Data source: CEIC)

First, in terms of economic growth sources, the contribution of consumption demand to GDP growth increased sharply under the background of the slowdown in investment and weak demand in the external market.

In 2015, the main factors behind the sharp slowdown of investment growth were excess production capacity in manufacturing and excess inventory in the real estate industry. The real investment in fixed assets (excluding farmers' investments) grew by 12.0 %, a decrease of 2.9 percentage points from the previous year. The contribution of annual capital formation to GDP growth fell to 36.1 %, a decrease of 11.2 percentage points from the previous year. On the other hand, urban and rural residents' real income growth continued to slow, but growth in consumption was relatively stable. The real total retail sales of consumption goods grew by 10.6 %, a decrease of 0.3 percentage points from the previous year. The contribution of final consumption to economic growth rose from 51 % in 2014 to 66.4 % (see Fig. 1.2).

It's worth noting that, during the deceleration of China's economy as a result of the Asian financial crisis, the contribution of final consumption to economic growth was close to 80 % in 1999 and 2000. From 2002 to 2007, China's economy entered a new period of high growth, but the contribution of final consumption to economic growth continued to decrease and was subdued for a long time, due mainly to the relatively slow increase in Chinese residents' income and the continued slowdown of residents' marginal propensity to consume over 10 years ago. After 2010, because of the global financial crisis, China's economy slowed again. At that time, although Chinese residents' real income grew at a rate similar to that of economic growth, the contribution of final consumption to economic growth never exceeded the level in Asian financial crisis. This shows that it's far from easy to

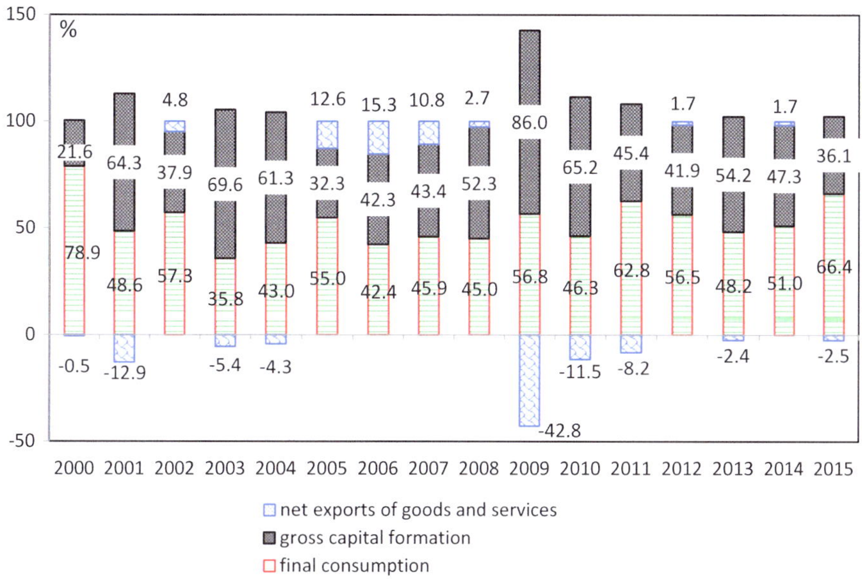

Fig. 1.2 Changes in contribution rate of GDP growth based on the expenditure accounting approach (Data source: CEIC)

reach the new economic growth path of "domestic demand-oriented, consumption-driven" after undergoing an economic growth pattern of high investment, high exports, and low consumption for a long time.

Second, the industrial structure adjusted in a timely way through per capita income improvement and demand structure transformation. The tertiary industry's share of GDP increased by 2.4 percentage points in 2015, reaching 50.5 %, 10.0 percentage points higher than the share of the secondary industry (see Fig. 1.3). The tertiary industry's share continued to rise, ensuring a somewhat stable employment situation for the whole year.[1]

However, contrary to developed countries like the US, labor productivity in the tertiary industry was lower than in the secondary industry for a long time up until now.[2] As the gravity center of China's economy gradually shifted from the secondary industry to the tertiary industry, the low labor productivity of the tertiary

[1]Although the economic growth of China continued to decline, 11 million new jobs were generated for urban residents in 2015, exceeding the target of 10 million new jobs set in early 2015, and slightly higher than 10.70 million in 2014; at the same time, reduction in the supply of labor force also eased the pressure on employment to a certain extent. By the end of 2015, the population for mainland China is 1.37462 billion, an increase of 6.8 million person than the previous year. Person aged 16–59 years (including those below 60 years), the working-age population, totaled 910.96 million people; this was 4.87 million persons less than the previous year, share of the total population of 66.3 %.

[2]See Center for Macroeconomic Research of Xiamen University, China's Macroeconomic Outlook, quarterly Forecast and Analysis Report (autumn of 2015).

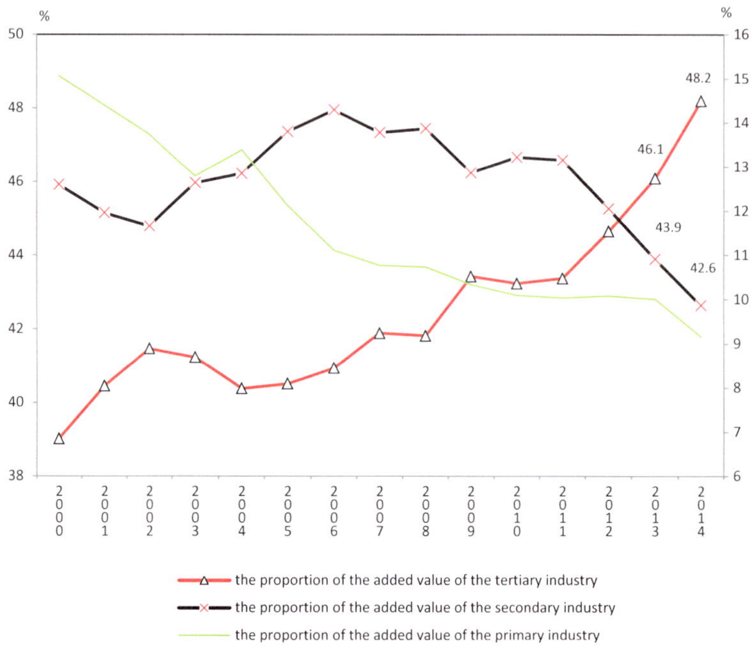

Fig. 1.3 Changes in proportion of added value of three industries in GDP (Data source: CEIC)

industry not only reduced the potential growth rate of the economy but also directly restrained residents' income from rapid improvement. Several tasks are critical to ensuring that China's economy develops stably and quickly and promoting economic growth pattern reform in the next decade: adjusting industrial structure with demand structure transformation, adjusting the interior structure of the primary and secondary industry, improving product quality and grade, reducing cost while simultaneously raising the share of the modern service sector, pursuing deregulation, breaking down access barriers, and facilitating market competition to promote the labor productivity of the tertiary industry as soon as possible.

Third, private investment growth fell sharply, hindering the structural improvement of China's investments. From 2011 to 2014, private fixed assets investment growth was always faster than total fixed asset investment growth, and the proportion of private investment out of total fixed assets investment also continued to increase, showing that the investment structure improved consistently.[3] Private investment began to become the main support of investments in fixed assets growth for high investment efficiency and stable economic growth. However, private investment grew by only 10.1 % in 2015, a sharp decrease of 6.9 percentage points from the previous year. The proportion of private investment out of total fixed

[3]See the Center for Macroeconomic Research at Xiamen University, China's Macroeconomic Outlook, quarterly Forecast and Analysis Report (autumn 2015).

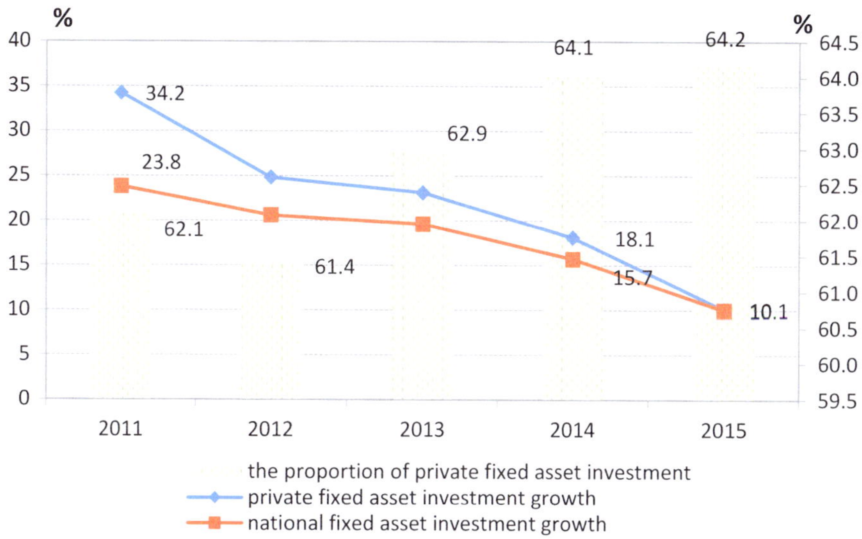

Fig. 1.4 Changes in growth rate and proportion of investment in private fixed assets (Data source: CEIC)

assets investment in 2015 was 64.2 %, a slight increase of 0.1 percentage points from the previous year (see Fig. 1.4). Private investment growth showed a sharp decline, hindering the structural improvement of China's investment, and improvement ground to a halt. In the background of the easy monetary policy in 2015, the sharp decline of private investment growth was caused by many factors. Besides demand factors, several problems deserved to be urgently explored, such as whether increased credit resources were allocated to the real economy effectively, whether they flowed to the private economy and satisfied demand, whether the private economy expanded effectively, and whether visible and invisible barriers were removed.

Fourth, manufacturing investment growth continued to decline, and industrial structure transformation was slow. The transformation and upgrading of manufacturing are critical for China to promote labor productivity and build advantages in international competition in the next stage. Industrial structure adjustment has progressed gradually over the past few years, with a slowdown in investment. Sharply reducing investments in overcapacity industries and continuously increasing investment in the high-tech industry promoted the transformation and promotion of manufacturing; however, this process began to slow because of the slowdown in investment in 2015. The added value of manufacturing grew by 7.0 %, a decrease of 2.4 percentage points from the previous year. Of this amount, the added value of general equipment manufacturing grew by 2.9 %, a decrease of 6.2 percentage points from the previous year. The added value of special equipment manufacturing grew by 3.4 %, a decrease of 3.5 percentage points from the previous year. The added value of railway, shipbuilding, aerospace and other transportation equipment manufacturing sectors grew by 6.8 %, a decrease of 5.9 percentage points from the previous year. Computers, communications and other electronic equipment manufacturing grew by 10.5 %, a decrease of 1.7 percentage points from the previous year.[4]

By comparison, private investment made an obvious contribution to the transformation and promotion of manufacturing. In 2015, although private investment growth declined sharply, the industrial structure of private investment continued to improve: the proportion of investment in the secondary industry decreased stably, and the proportion of investment in computers, communications and other electronic equipment manufacturing consistently increased simultaneously. Investment in manufacturing grew by 9.1 % in 2015, a decrease of 7.7 percentage points from the previous year, and the proportion of private investment in manufacturing was 89.4 %, a decrease of 0.2 percentage points from the previous year. Of this share, the proportion of investment in general equipment was 7.89 %, and the proportion of investment in special equipment manufacturing was 7.08 %, an increase of 0.2 and 0.1 percentage points from the previous year, respectively; the proportion of investment in railway, shipbuilding, aerospace and other transportation equipment manufacturing was 1.4 %, a decrease of 0.2 percentage points from the previous year; the proportion of investment in computers, communications, and other electronic equipment manufacturing was 3.8 %, an increase of 0.2 percentage points from the previous year.

Finally, energy-saving and cost-reduction made new progress. The energy consumption out of unit GDP decreased by 5.6 % in 2015, an increase of 0.8 percentage points from the decrease in the previous year and an increase of 1.9 percentage points from the decrease in 2013.

1.2 Fixed Asset Investment Growth Fell Overall, and the Improvement of the Investment Structure Was Blocked

Investment fell overall in 2015. Manufacturing and real estate investment growth fell consistently, leading to a corresponding sharp decline in the growth of total social fixed asset investment, and almost all of the other industries suffered slow growth. In terms of industrial structure, investment in the primary, secondary, and tertiary industries grew by 31.8 %, 8 %, and 10.6 % respectively, a decrease of 2.1, 5.2, and 6.2 percentage points from the previous year respectively. In the secondary industry, influenced by excess capacity, investment in the mining industry grew by

[4]According to China's National Bureau of Statistics, new industry grew rapidly, and the added value of high-tech industry grew by 10.2 %, an increase of 4.1 percentage points faster than the industries above the designated scale, representing 11.8 % of the industries above the designated scale, an increase of 1.2 percentage points over the previous year.

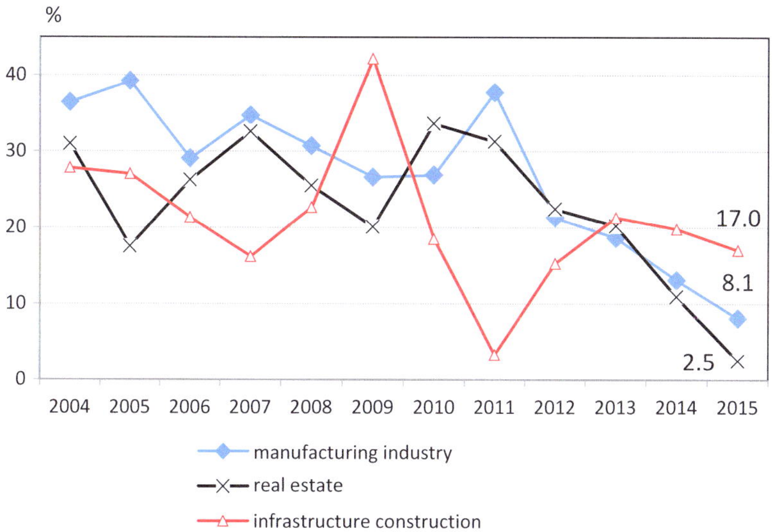

Fig. 1.5 Changes in growth rate of investment in fixed assets by industry (Data source: CEIC)

−8.8 %, a decrease of 9.5 percentage points from the previous year. Investment in manufacturing grew by 8.1 %, a decrease of 5.4 percentage points from the previous year. Investment in electricity, heating power, gas and water production, and the supply industry grew by 16.6 %, a decrease of 0.5 percentage points from the previous year. In the tertiary industry, influenced by excess inventory, investment in real estate grew by 2.5 %, a sharp decrease of 8.6 percentage points from the previous year.[5] Investment in transportation, warehousing, and postal services grew by 14.3 %, a decrease of 4.3 percentage points from the previous year (see Fig. 1.5).

Investment growth in manufacturing and real estate reduced the proportion of these two industries out of total investment. In 2015, manufacturing investment accounted for 32.7 % of total investment, a decrease of 0.6 percentage points from the previous year; real estate investment accounted for 23.0 % of total investment, a decrease of 1.6 percentage points from the previous year; and infrastructure construction investment accounted for 23.8 %,[6] an increase of 1.4 percentage points over the previous year.

In terms of the industrial structure of private investment, private investment in the primary industry grew by 33.1 % in 2015, a decrease of 1.9 percentage points from the previous year; this accounted for 3.6 % of total private investment, an

[5]According to China's National Bureau of Statistics, investment in national real estate development was 9.5979 trillion yuan in 2015, a nominal increase of 1.0 % from the previous year (real growth was 2.8 %).

[6]This included transportation, warehousing and postal services, water conservancy, environment and public facilities management, electricity, heating power, gas and water production, and the supply industry.

increase of 0.6 percentage points over the previous year. Private investment in the secondary industry grew by 9.4 %, a decrease of 7.3 percentage points from the previous year; this accounted for 50.1 % of total private investment, a decrease of 0.3 percentage points from the previous year. Private investment in the tertiary industry grew by 9.4 %, a decrease of 9.2 percentage points from the previous year; this accounted for 46.4 % of total private investment, a decrease of 0.3 percentage points from the previous year.

In terms of investment sources, investment from all kinds of ownership enterprises showed declining growth. Investment from domestic enterprises grew by 10.6 %, a 5.7 percentage point reduction from the previous year (see Fig. 1.6). Among domestic enterprises, investment from state-owned and state-holding enterprises grew by 10.9 %, a 2.1 percentage point reduction from the previous year; investment from private investment grew by 10.1 %, a sharp fall of 6.9 percentage points from the previous year. Investment from enterprises located in Hong Kong, Macao, and Taiwan grew by 0, a 8.7 percentage point reduction from the previous year; investment from foreign enterprises grew by 2.8 %, a 2.5 percentage point reduction from the previous year. Although investment from all investment sources showed declining growth, investment from private investment, enterprises located in Hong Kong, Macao, and Taiwan and foreign enterprises showed sharper declining growth than investment from state-owned and state-holding enterprises, which clearly showed the weak demand in China's economy in 2015.

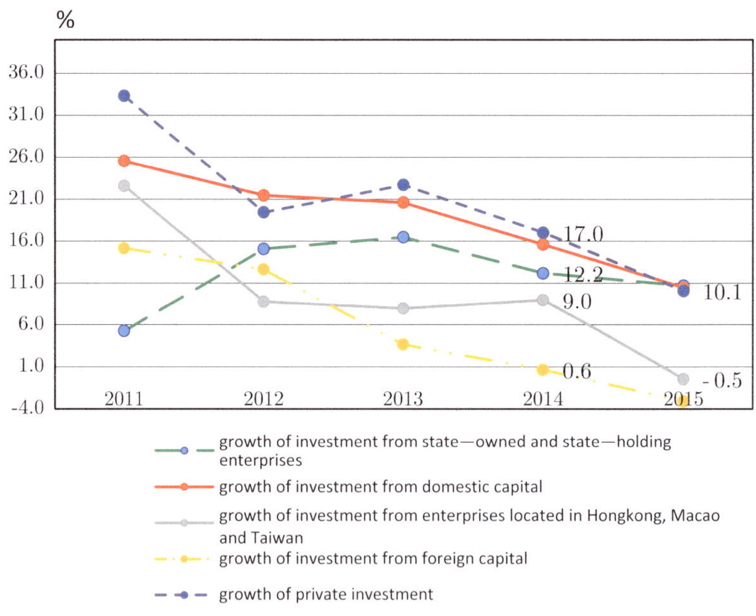

Fig. 1.6 Nominal growth of fixed asset investment year on year (by investment source) (Data source: CEIC)

In terms of capital source, investment from national budget funds grew by 15.6 % in 2015, an increase of 1.5 percentage points over the previous year; this accounted for 5.6 % of total investment, a decrease of 0.5 percentage points from the previous year. Investment from domestic loans grew by −5.8 %, a sharp decrease of 14.4 percentage points from the previous year; this accounted for 11.0 % of total investment, a decrease of 1.8 percentage points from the previous year. Investment from self-raised funds grew by 9.5 %, a decrease of 4.9 percentage points from the previous year; this accounted for 73.4 % of total investment, a decrease of 0.3 percentage points from the previous year.

The main factors behind the sharp slowdown of total fixed asset investment in 2015 was the continued decline of investment growth in manufacturing and the real estate industry; in terms of industry structure changes, however, investment showed an industry-wide slowdown. This indicated the weak demand in China's economy. In terms of changes in investment and capital sources, growth of private investment and investment from domestic loans showed a sharp slowdown, indicating that the quantitative easing policy didn't allocate credit resources to the real economy effectively, especially to the private economy sectors of the real economy. In terms of capital supply, amid the decelerating economy, deflation in the production sector (continued fall of PPI), and the increased real burden of enterprise debt, the financial sector stinted on loans because of the raised risk, which restrained the expansion of effective investment demand.

Moreover, China's capital market is imperfect, the scale of its enterprise bond market is too small, stock prices fall when bubbles burst in the stock market, and the central bank strictly supervises off-balance sheet activities. All these factors make it difficult for enterprises, especially private enterprises, to acquire investment capital even if they have investment demand. There are also still many restrictions, visible and invisible, on private investment, hindering private investment in continuously expanding industries with increased income and demand structure adjustments. During China's transition period, the supply for these industries is inadequate because of institutional barriers, government regulation, monopolies, and the lagging market-oriented reform.

We believe that weak demand is the main reason for the continued slowdown of the economy. Demand is shrinking for the following reasons. First, when foreign demand shrinks, domestic demand (consumption demand) can't expand quickly due to a slowdown in income growth. Second, to cope with shocks from the international finance crisis, after the implementation of the "four trillion yuan" investment stimulus plan, the expansion of infrastructure and the superfast expansion of the real estate industry led to excess production capacity in capital goods industries like armored concrete manufacturing. Meanwhile, the excess expansion of some emerging industries (like the solar photovoltaic industry) was stimulated for steady growth, which restrained growth in investment demand.[7] Third,

[7]We can't ignore the role of state-owned and state-holding enterprises.

structural deflation has restrained enterprises' profit growth and increased their debt burden while restraining growth in investment demand.

However, the current slowdown of investment demand should be short-term in the transition period because current "excess" supply is largely structural excess, as China is transitioning from an average- or above average-income economy to a developed economy, leading to improvements in average personal income, an unbalanced supply–demand structure during the transformation of the demand structure, and a vast and serious supply shortage. Along with the reform in the supply structure, with the rejection of excess production capacity and reduced ineffective investments (subtraction), the supply shortage was exposed during the demand transformation, which would inevitably stimulate new effective supply and investment demand (addition) under the drag of the market. During this process, all that can satisfy the demand effectively is the main body of the market economy: the private market. During the slowdown of China's economy, the fact that the proportion of private investment out of total investment is consistently rising illustrates that not only are there many kinds of investment opportunities in China's economy during this process of structural transformation but also that investment efficiency is continuously improving along with improvements in the proportion of private investment. However, the limitations of market-oriented reform, imperfections in the capital market, the lag in financial system reform, and systematic obstacles are blocking the stable expansion of the private economy and keeping the economy from adjusting to the transformation of the demand structure more sensitively, adjusting to the investment structure more quickly, improving investment efficiency, and stabilizing economy growth.

1.3 Import and Export Growth Fell Sharply, but the Trade Structure Continued to Improve

In 2015, the global economic recovery was weak. The IMF estimates that global trade in goods and services grew by 2.6 % in 2015, a decrease of 0.8 percentage points from 2014.[8] Under this impact, China's export growth fell further. At the same time, affected by weak domestic demand and the decline in the prices of oil and other staple commodities, import growth fell sharply, and the decline in import growth was larger than the decline in export growth. The surplus in commodity trade increased sharply in 2015. China's annual total exports in USD grew by −2.8 %, a decrease of 8.9 percentage points from the previous year; its total imports grew by −14.1 %, a decrease of 14.5 percentage points from the previous year (see Fig. 1.7). China's commodity trade surplus expanded significantly to 593 billion USD, an increase of 209.94 billion USD over the previous year.

[8]According to the IMF World Economic Outlook. Growth in 2016 is predicted to be back to 3.4 %, and growth in 2017 is predicted to rise to 4.1 %.

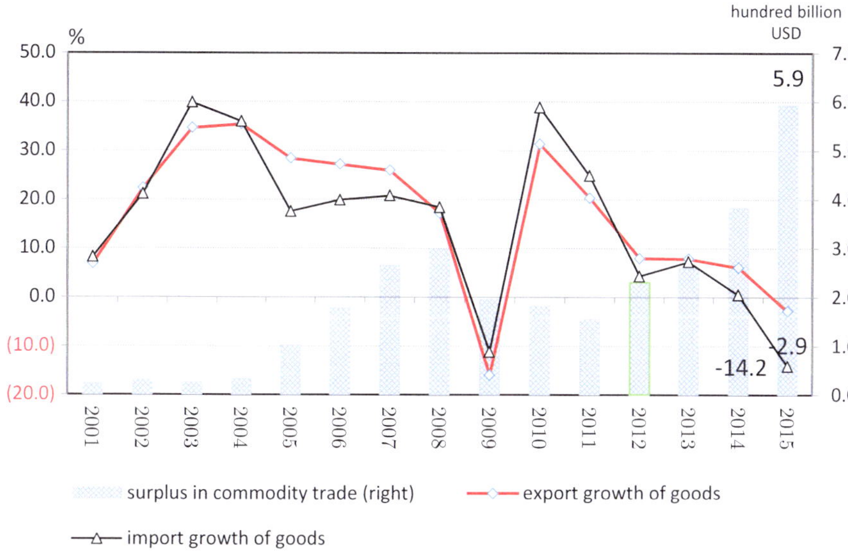

Fig. 1.7 Changes in import and export growth and trade surplus scale (Data source: CEIC)

In terms of trade structure, the proportion of general trade continued to improve. In 2015, general trade exports grew by 1.4 %, a decrease of 9.3 percentage points from the previous year; this accounted for 53.7 % of total exports, a 2.3 % increase over the previous year. Processing trade exports grew by −9.7 %, a decrease of 12.4 percentage points from the previous year; this accounted for 35.1 % of total exports, a 2.7 % decrease from the previous year. The general trade import growth fell from 0.2 to −16.8 %, accounting for 54.9 % of total imports, a decrease of 1.8 percentage points from the previous year. Growth of processing trade imports fell from 5.7 to −14.9 %, accounting for 26.6 % of total imports, a decrease of 0.2 percentage points from the previous year (see Fig. 1.8). The annual surplus of general trade was 296.68 billion USD, an increase of 203.69 billion USD in scale from the previous year. The annual surplus of processing trade was 353.07 billion USD, a decrease of 5.7 billion USD in scale from the previous year. The scale of the surplus in processing trade was still larger than that of general trade.

In 2015, with the expansion of the commodity trade surplus, the services trade deficit continued to expand. By the third quarter of 2015, the services trade deficit had expanded to 66.25 billion USD. It's worth noting that the ratio of the commodity trade surplus and services trade deficit showed a sharp decline since 2010 (see Fig. 1.9). China's commodity trade surplus was 10.5 times the services trade deficit in 2015, dropping to 4.9 times in 2011, to 3.9 times in 2012, to 2.9 times in 2013 and 2014, and to 2.6 times by the third quarter of 2015. The relatively small services trade deficit has led to a continued surplus in China's current account.

In the long run, the rise in domestic income will cause China's export-orientated processing trade to lose its comparative advantage, and the commodity trade

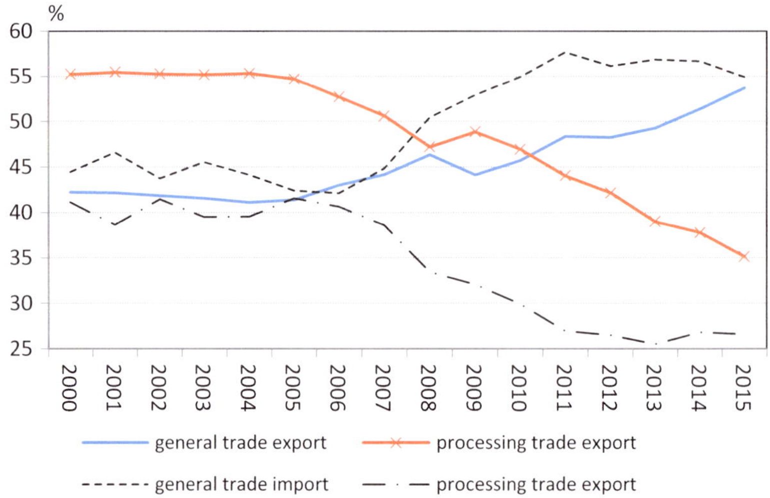

Fig. 1.8 Changes in proportion of general trade and processing trade import and export (Data source: CEIC)

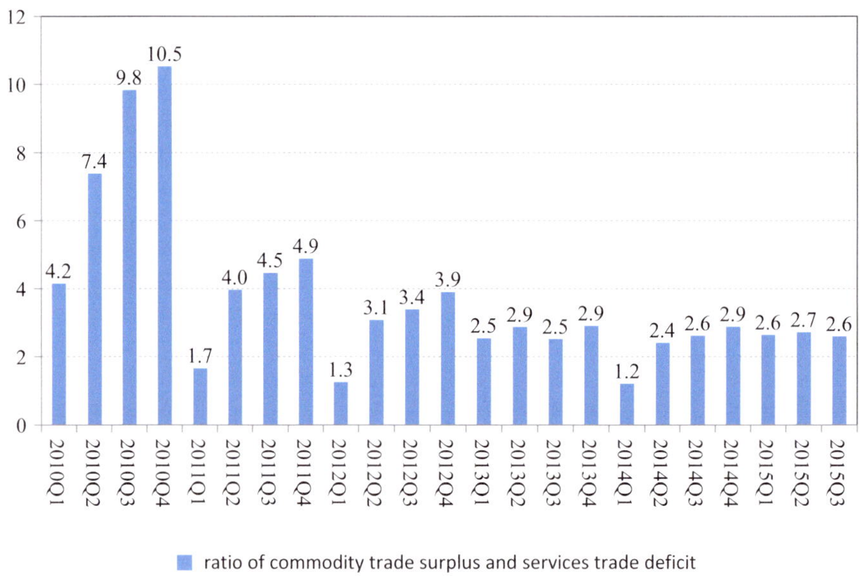

Fig. 1.9 Comparison on scale of commodity trade surplus and services trade deficit (Data source: CEIC)

surplus will rely on the import and export of general trade; this is the necessary condition for an economy to transit from a high-growth developing economy to a developed economy, and is also a normal condition for industrial structure upgrading. At the same time, the scale of China's overseas direct investment

(ODI) is still small compared with its incoming FDI, although it has increased rapidly over the past few years. In the foreseeable future, investment revenue from China's service trade will maintain a deficit and expand. Therefore, in the next stage, if China's export-orientated manufacturing can't upgrade its export goods and form a new export competition advantage, the surplus condition of the current account will soon be inverted.

In terms of regional structure, China's growth in exports to Asia and the US (in USD) grew in 2015 by −4 % and 3.4 %, respectively, a decrease of 8.8 and 4.1 percentage points from the previous year, respectively. Following the euro depreciation and the slowdown of the EU recovery, exports to the EU increased by 1.7 %, a decrease of 3.2 percentage points from the previous year (see Fig. 1.10a). Compared with 2014, China's exports to Asia accounted for 50.1 %, a decrease of 0.6 %; its exports to the US and the EU accounted for 18 % and 15.5 %, an increase of 1.1 % and 0.7 %, respectively (see Fig. 1.11a). On the import side, China's growth of imports from Asia and the US fell to −12 % and −6.5 %, a decrease of 11.6 % and 10.9 %, respectively; its growth of imports from the EU decreased significantly to −15.5 %, a decrease of 30.9 % (see Fig. 1.10b). The proportion of China's imports from Asia increased by 1.4 %, reaching 56.8 %; the proportion from the US increased by 0.7 %, reaching 8.8 %; and the proportion from the EU was 11.6 %, the same general level as that of the previous year (see Fig. 1.11b).

In terms of capital flow, the scale of China's use of foreign capital decreased slightly. In 2015, the use of foreign capital was 126.27 billion USD, a decrease of 2.24 billion USD from the previous year. On the other hand, China's outward FDI grew fast. In 2015, the scale of direct non-financial investment in 6532 overseas enterprises was 118.02 billion USD, an increase of 14.7 % year to year. Of this amount, investment in the US and the ASEAN grew fastest, an increase of 60.1 % and 60.7 % year to year, respectively. Outward FDI in the "One Belt and One Road"

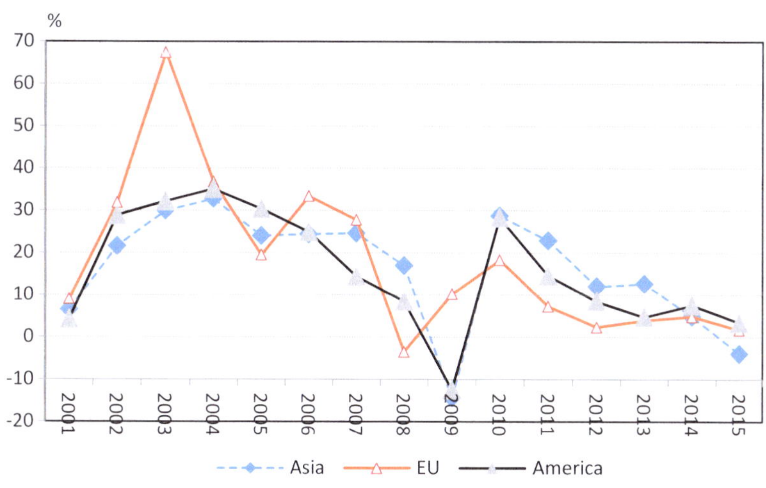

Fig. 1.10a Changes in China's export growth in main areas (Data source: CEIC)

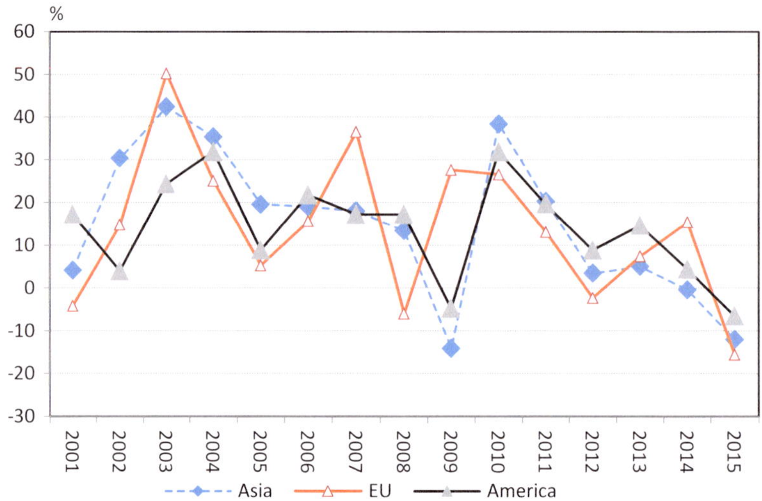

Fig. 1.10b Changes in China's import growth in main areas (Data source: CEIC)

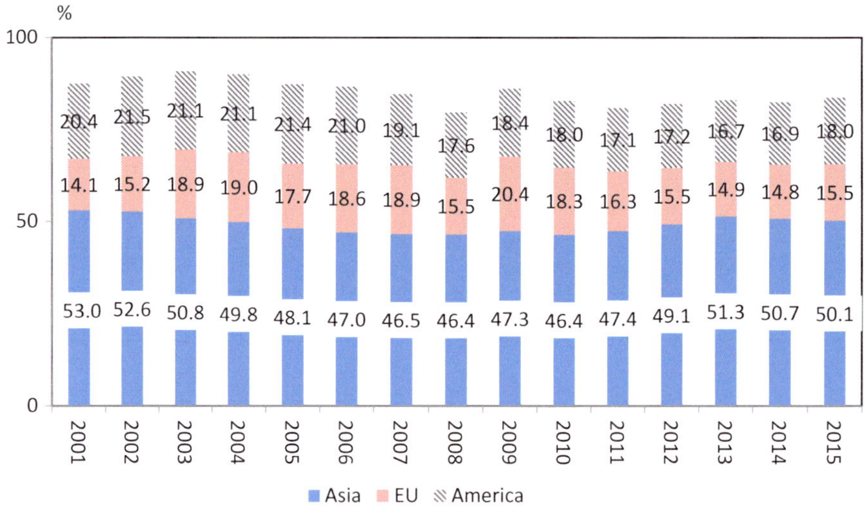

Fig. 1.11a Structure changes in China's export (By region) (Data source: CEIC)

(OBOR) region also grew fast; we invested directly in 49 OBOR nations, for a total investment of 14.82 billion USD, an increase of 18.2 % year to year, accounting for 12.6 % of total investment.[9]

[9]Data from the Ministry of Commerce's website.

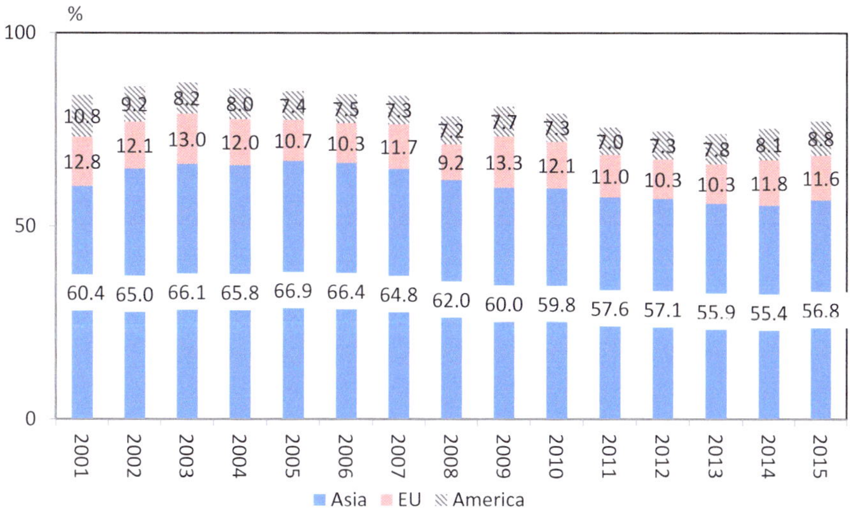

Fig. 1.11b Structure changes in China's import (By region) (Data source: CEIC)

Finally, in terms of the RMB exchange rate, the People's Bank of China began a reform to complete the bidding mechanism of the central parity exchange rate of the RMB, and the RMB showed a sharp depreciation against the dollar. At the end of the year, the central parity exchange rate was 6.4936 yuan to the dollar, indicating an RMB depreciation of 6.0 % compared to the end of the previous year. At the beginning of 2016, the expectation of a further increase in dollar interest rates and a depreciation of the RMB resulting from the domestic economic slowdown strengthened the tendency of capital outflow. In 2015, annual accumulated foreign exchange reserves decreased by 512.26 billion USD, the largest annual decline on record, finally reaching 3.33 trillion USD.

1.4 Slowdown in Residents' Real Income Growth and Steady Increase in Consumption

In 2015, Chinese residents' per capita disposable income grew by 7.4 % in real terms, a decrease of 0.6 % from the previous year, though higher than the per capita personal GDP growth rate (6.9 %). The per capita disposable income of urban residents grew by 6.6 % in real terms, a decrease of 0.2 % from the previous year; the per capita disposable income of rural residents grew by 7.5 %, a decrease of 1.7 % from the previous year (see Fig. 1.12). **The constant economic slowdown continued to inhibit growth in urban and rural residents' real income; rural residents had higher real income growth yet a larger reduction range than urban residents.** On the other hand, consumption increased steadily. In 2015, the

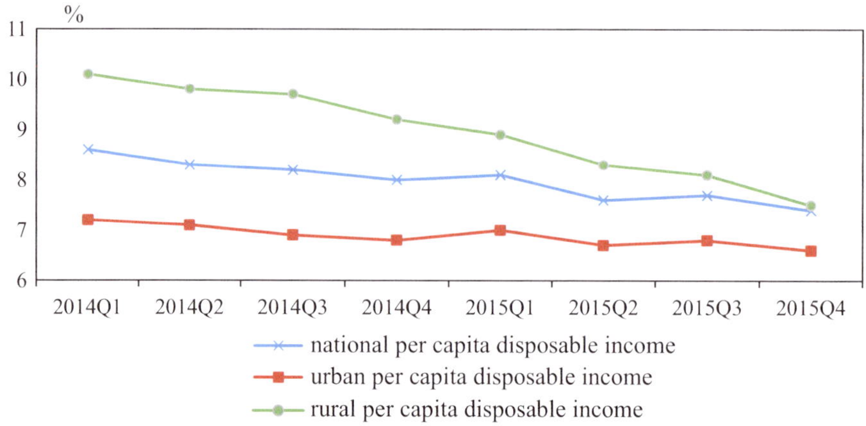

Fig. 1.12 Changes in growth rate of national per capita disposable income (Data source: CEIC)

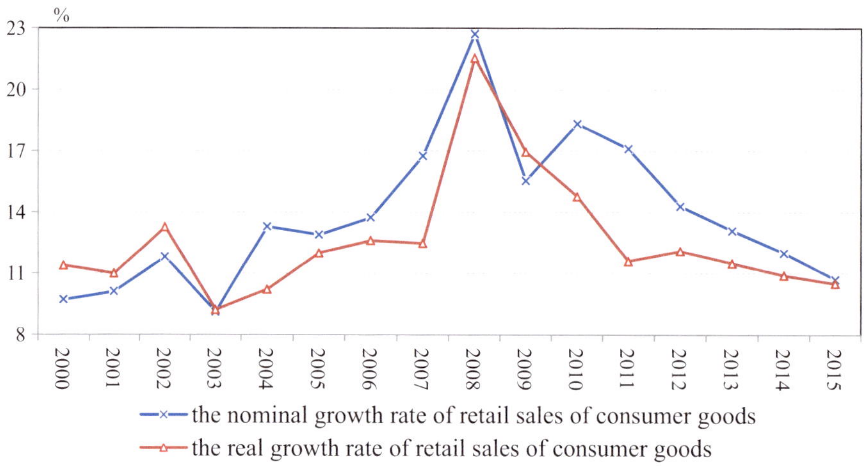

Fig. 1.13 Changes in growth rate of consumer good retail sales (Data source: CEIC)

total retail sales of consumption goods grew by 10.7 % nominally, a decrease of 1.3 % from the previous year; meanwhile, real growth was 10.5 %, a decrease of 0.4 % from the previous year (see Fig. 1.13).

1.5 Price Index Continued the "Double Down" Trend, and Structural Deflation Was Increasing

The CPI growth rate was 1.4 % in 2015, 0.6 % lower than that of the previous year; the PPI was −5. 2 %, 3.3 % greater than the previous year's decreasing amplitude (see Fig. 1.14); The GDP deflator was −0.4 %, a decrease of 1.27 %

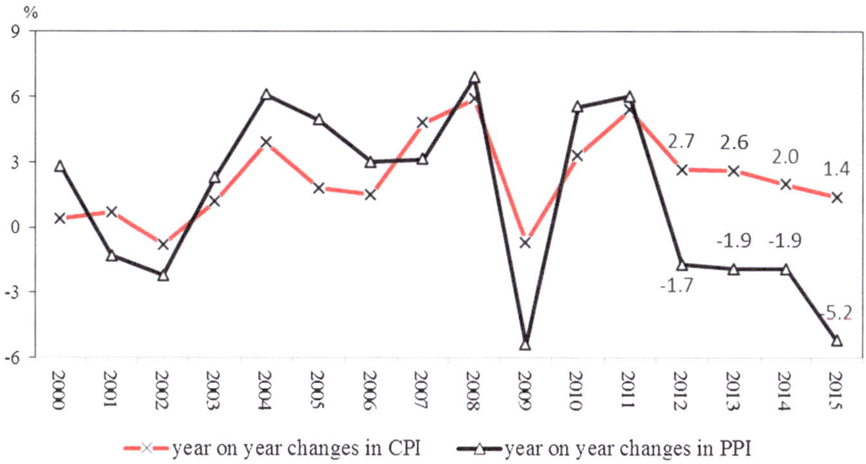

Fig. 1.14 Year-on-year changes in CPI and PPI (Data source: CEIC)

from 2014.[10] Since 2012, China's CPI and PPI have continued the "double down" trend, but CPI growth remained slightly positive, whereas that of PPI continued an expanding negative trend. **The consumer market, intermediate product market, and investment product market faced different downward pressures on price, and the deflation revealed obvious structural characteristics.**

In terms of CPI, eight types of consumer goods maintained their positive increase, although all rates of increase dropped. The falling prices of staple commodities such as food and oil was the main reason for this drop; the increasing demand for services, clothing, traffic, communication, entertainment, education, and culture, together with a lag in market-oriented reform, promoted the sustained CPI uptrend. In terms of PPI, excess production capacity in part of the domestic upstream manufacturing industry and the 2014 slump in global oil prices were the main causes for the drop.

The structural deflation since 2012 was caused by the large scale of capacity motivation (including real estate expansion) during the global financial crisis. However, systemic factors made it hard to cut the overcapacity.[11] The result was aggravated structural deflation. The continual drop in PPI has already imposed the following negative macroeconomic effects:

1. Continued decline in manufacturing industry profit[12];
2. Reduced fiscal revenue growth directly related to manufacturing industry profit;
3. Widened expansionary development gap between districts;

[10]Measured by team.

[11]Mainly because of the lack of effective disposal measures for state-owned "zombie" enterprises.

[12]In 2015, the profits of the abovementioned industrial enterprises grew by −2.3 %, a decrease of 5.6 percentage points from the previous year.

4. Higher risk of comprehensive deflation;
5. Heavier real debt burden for enterprises.

Considering the current shrinking demand and severe overcapacity, it's obviously necessary to make good use of the low PPI and investment price to augment investment and increase demand and capacity utilization to prevent a further drop in the economy's growth rate. However, one important lesson learned from the macroeconomic policy practiced in 2008 is that it's impossible for the government to expand domestic demand by replicating the "four trillion stimulation plan" and enhancing infrastructure. A targeted solution for the economic growth slowdown ought to be rooted in a systemic analysis of China's demand, supply, structure, institutions, economy, and society.

1.6 The Monetary Policy Generally Eased, but Offered Limited Promotion of Investment

In 2015, the monetary policies were generally eased. The reserve requirement ratio (RRR) decreased by 2.5 percentage points from 19.5 to 17.0 % after five cuts (including targeted ones). Meanwhile, five cuts of the benchmark interest rate for loans reduced it by 1.25 percentage points from 5.6 to 4.35 %. The 1-year deposit rate fell by 1 % as well. These measures led to a 1.21 % decline in the one-year benchmark interest rate for loans, from 5.51 to 4.30 % by the end of December (see Fig. 1.15). However, the interbank market rate reached its lowest in the middle of the year, then started to rebound (on monthly weighted averages): the interbank

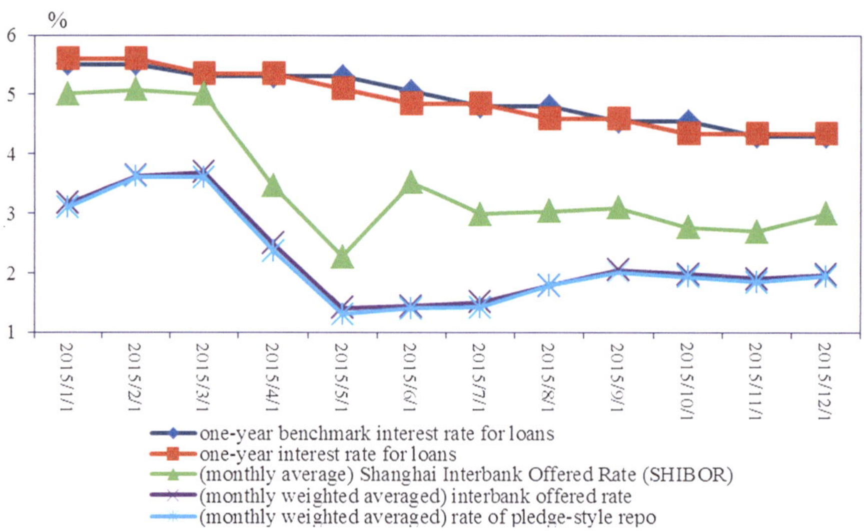

Fig. 1.15 Changes in varied kinds of market rates (Data source: CEIC)

offered rate dropped from 3.18 % in January to its lowest of 1.42 % in May, then rose to 1.97 % in December; the annual total decline range was 1.2 %; the rate of pledge-style repo started from 3.103 % in January, fell to its lowest of 1.305 % in May, then returned to 1.946 % in December, for a yearly drop of 1.16 %; similarly, the monthly average Shanghai Interbank Offered Rate (SHIBOR) was 5.01 % in January, shifted to 3.002 % in December, and dropped to 2.276 % in May, for an overall decline of 2.01 percentage points.

In 2015, currency in circulation (M0) grew by 4.9 %, an increase of 2 percentage points from the previous year. Narrow money (M1) grew by 15.2 %, an increase of 12 % from the previous year. Broad money (M2) grew by 13.3 %, a decrease of 1.1 % from 2014. M2 increased by 16.39 trillion yuan, an expansion of 4.21 trillion yuan from the previous year. M2 was ultimately 139.23 trillion yuan, twice as large as the annual GDP in 2015.

In 2015, the scale of social financing was 15.4 trillion yuan, 104.7 billion yuan less than the previous year (see Fig. 1.16). The newly increased RMB loans amounted to 11.27 trillion yuan, an increase of 1.94 trillion yuan over the previous year, accounting for 73.2 % of the scale of social financing for the same period, 13.7 % higher than the previous year. Of the newly increased RMB loans, 63 % was used to finance nonfinancial companies and other departments, 3.2 % less than the previous year, while 30.6 % was used to finance the real estate sector, 2.5 percentage points higher than the previous year.

In terms of finance supply, strict regulation of shadow banks led to a sharp shrinkage of bank trust loans, which restrained increases in the social financing scale.[13] Although newly increased RMB credit grew rapidly in the first half-year,

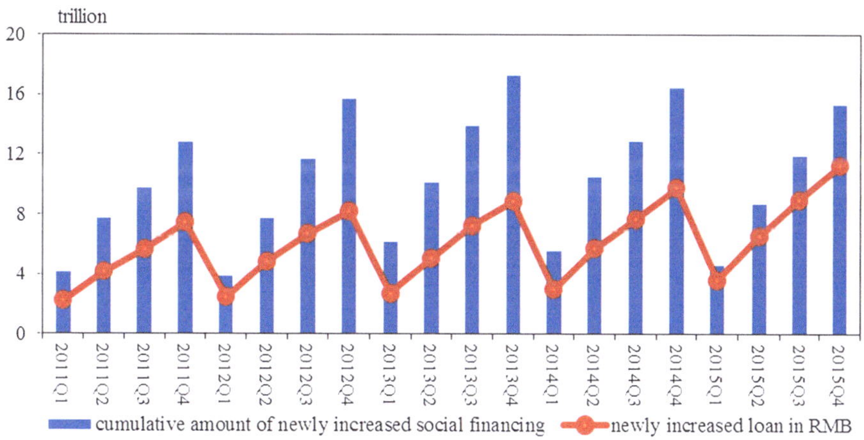

Fig. 1.16 Cumulative amount of newly increased social financing and newly increased loan in RMB (Data source: CEIC)

[13]In 2015, regulators restricted the expansion of commercial banks' off-balance sheet activities and social financial scale by regulating the inter-bank business standard. Trust loans accounted for 0.28 % of the total social finance, a decrease of 2.82 percentage points from the previous year.

the enormous decline in private investment growth showed that the resource allocation mechanism, which depended on indirect financing, was still not conducive to the expansion of investment demand. Now, that off-balance loans including trust loans were restrained, direct financing was limited, and monetary policies have improved interbank flexibility and saved financial costs. However, this did not ease the "unavailable and expensive financing" for private investment. Thus, how to improve credit resource allocation efficiency—in other words, how to satisfy private investment demand expansion with newly increased credit resources—was still the main problem facing our finance system.

1.7 Fiscal Revenue Growth Was Falling, but the Fiscal Expenditure Structure Continued to Improve

In 2015, China's fiscal revenue grew by 8.4 %, a decrease of 0.2 % from the previous year. Fiscal expenditure grew by 15.8 %, an increase of 7.6 % from the previous year[14] (see Fig. 1.17). The financial deficit was 2.3551 trillion yuan, accounting for 3.5 % of GDP.

In terms of fiscal revenue, the decline in corporate profit growth inhibited the increase of tax revenue. Annual tax revenue grew by 4.8 %, a decrease of 3 % from the previous year; the ratio of tax revenue to financial revenue was 82.0 %, a decrease of 2.9 % from the previous year. Meanwhile, the non-tax revenue

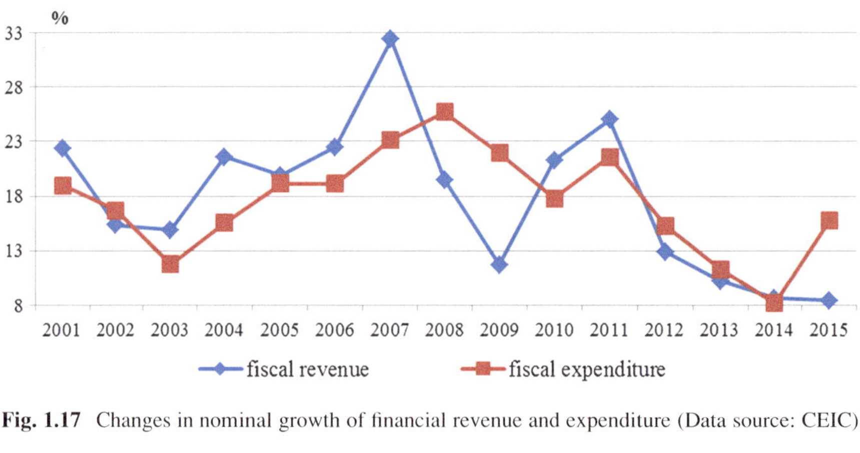

Fig. 1.17 Changes in nominal growth of financial revenue and expenditure (Data source: CEIC)

[14]In 2015, general public budget revenue was 15.2217 trillion yuan; the growth rate, which was below the initial budget target, slowed to 8.4 %, or even 5.8 % at the same caliber, a decrease of 2.8 % from the previous year. General public budget spending was 17.5768 trillion yuan, an increase of 15.8 %, or 13.2 % at the same caliber, from the previous year, and 4.9 % higher in terms of growth rate.

increased by 28.9 % and its growth rate increased by 15.4 % while the growth of tax revenue decreased. Income from the transfer of state-owned land use rights was 3.25 trillion yuan, one trillion yuan less than the previous year.

On the side of fiscal spending, education spending grew by 8.4 %, an increase of 4.3 % over the previous year. This accounted for 14.9 % of fiscal expenditure, a decrease of 0.2 % from the previous year. Social security and employment expenditure grew by 16.9 %, an increase of 7.1 % over the previous year; this accounted for 10.8 % of fiscal expenditure, an increase of 0.3 % over the previous year. Expenditure on medical treatment, public health, and family planning was 1.1916 trillion, an increase of 17.1 %. Expenditure on transportation and forestry and water affairs grew by 21.4 %, an increase of 14 % over the previous year; this accounted for 16.8 % of fiscal expenditure, an increase of 0.8 % over the previous year. In 2015, the proportion of education spending out of GDP approached 4 %, and the proportion of expenditure on social security or employment and medical treatment, public health or family planning out of GDP approached 3 % and 2 % respectively (see Fig. 1.18). This indicated that fiscal expenditures on people's livelihoods did not decline, although growth in fiscal revenue declined sharply in 2015.

Thus, China's economic growth slowed constantly in 2015. In the short term, weak demand was the main cause. First, to cope with the international financial crisis, the continual 2-year super-expansion in 2010 and 2011 of the real estate industry caused by the "four trillion stimulation plan" led to overcapacity in the production goods industry such as reinforced concrete and excessive stocks in real estate. Second, systemic factors made it hard to cut the overcapacity, and the results were aggravated by structural deflation, while the shrinking corporate profits directly inhibited their investment demand. Third, the continual slowdown in urban and rural residents' actual income growth restrained the expansion of

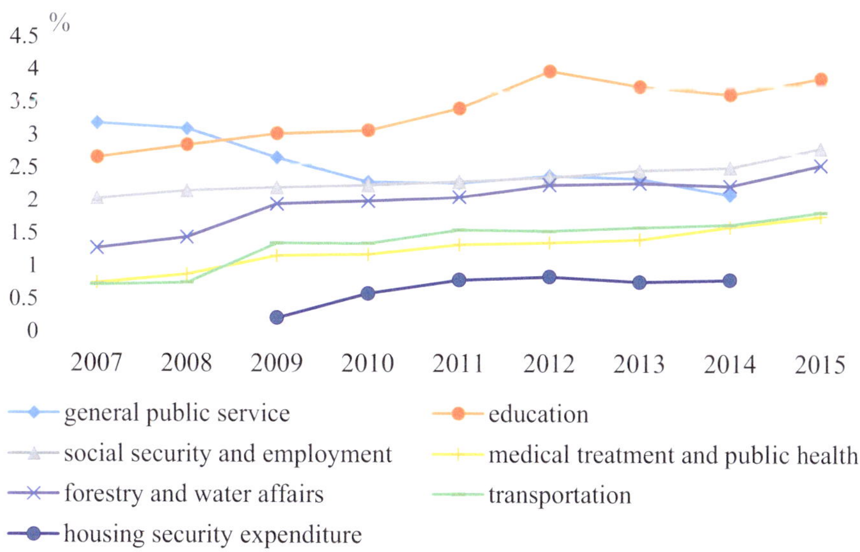

Fig. 1.18 Changes in public financial revenue and expenditure composition on GDP (Data source: CEIC)

consumption. In the background of a slowdown in investment and weakness in the foreign market, consumption demand contributed much more to the growth of GDP in 2015, but this contribution cannot compare with that in 1999 and 2000 after the Asian financial crisis. Fourth, the continual weakness of international market demand and the constant rise in domestic wages, which motivated the adjustment of the industrial structure, shrank the processing trade industry and export growth.

In the long run, the economic slowdown was the result of both the supply structure's encounter with increasing average personal income and the structural imbalance between supply and demand, accompanied by reduced production efficiency caused by the demand structure transformation. There were also important factors restricting economic development, including the imbalanced income allocation structure, the slow pace of market-oriented reform in the production factor market, the lagging and imperfect market-oriented reform in the capital market, and economic growth's failure to correspond with the transformation of the economic development stages.

The period covered by the 12th Five-year Plan came to a close in 2015, and the 13th plan started in 2016. Having summarized the experience of 2015 and expecting a beautiful 2016, our team proposes that the following issues deserve to be highlighted by the macroeconomic authorities.

First, under the huge downward pressure of the economy, the structural adjustment process began to slow. In terms of industrial structure, China's aggregate demand tended to rely on domestic demand rather than foreign demand. Meanwhile, as the per capita income level transited to that of a developed economy, China's domestic demand composition underwent profound change, with service products becoming as important as material products from the phase when the latter dominated; service products will soon play the main role. Therefore, the adjustment and upgrading of China's industrial structure will first be reflected by an evolution of the primary, secondary, and tertiary industries; the tertiary industry will have an increasing proportion. The secondary industry has behaved as the primary industry, corresponding to a decreased growth rate and proportion. The proportion of the tertiary industry out of GDP was over half, but, compared with the average level (55 %) of other countries with similar GDP per capita, it was still lower, with enormous room for development. More importantly, the tertiary industry mainly consists of traditional service industries with low labor productivity, while the modern service industry is seriously lagging due to the removal of government regulations and the promotion of marketization. As a result, the productivity and economy growth rate of the tertiary industry, as well as the national economy, were pulled down, and growth in personal income was restrained, as was consumption demand. Second, in terms of investment structure, despite insufficient demand, private investment growth fell sharply, and improvements in the investment structure slowed as the monetary policy eased. Investment funds from domestic loan growth fell sharply, meaning that the eased monetary policy did not allocate credit resources effectively to the real economy to satisfy private investment demand. At the same time, there are visible and invisible restrictions on and obstacles to private economy investment. Third, the expansion of the manufacturing scale slowed down, although structure upgrading was slow. General equipment manufacturing, special equipment manufacturing, railway, shipbuilding, aerospace and other transport equipment manufacturing, and computer communication and other electric equipment manufacturing industries grew at a declining rate.

Second, the **continual decline in economic growth led to a self-strengthening cycle of RMB devaluation expectation.** The People's Bank of China started to complete the reform of the central parity exchange rate quotation for the RMB against the dollar on August 11, 2015, and the RMB began to sharply devalue against the dollar. The current account maintained a surplus, but the shrinking scale of the actual use of foreign capital, the expanding scale of outbound investment, and the expectation of a further increase in USD interest, together with the RMB devaluation expectation caused by China's economic growth slowdown strengthened capital outflow pressure. The RMB devaluation expectation cycle finally took shape. First, to prevent the economy's liquidity from being squeezed out by a rapid decrease of foreign exchange reserves, the central bank had to cut RRR and benchmark interest rates to increase liquidity, which intensified the devaluation expectation and increased pressure on capital outflows. Second, the increased credit resources could not satisfy private investment demand, and inputted liquidity could not drive effective investment expansion due to the low efficiency of the financial system's allocation of credit resources and banks' "stinted loan" tendency. Thus, the measures of the central bank could not keep economic growth from falling but amplified the devaluation expectation. Third, in the RMB devaluation's promotion of export growth, there was not only a time lag but also a structural upgrading lag among China's export products, as well as uncertain demand in foreign markets; hence, devaluation could not stimulate exports and drive economic growth but just amplified the devaluation expectation. One key factor in this cycle is the stability of China's economic growth. Investment can be effectively stimulated by inputted liquidity to prevent a further drop in the economy if the efficiency of the finance system's credit resource allocation can be improved so that amplified resources can satisfy private investment demand.

Finally, for more than 4 years, the deflation in the industrial sector intensified due to limited cuts of overcapacity, which has already caused adverse effects on the macro economy. Continuously declining PPI severely restricted the growth of industry profits and fiscal revenue. Meanwhile, growth in several provinces that rely on natural resources has slowed sharply, which could cause even wider economic and social gaps between districts. Moreover, enterprises could face heavier real burdens. Cuts of overcapacity mean that the reemployment of the unemployed and the debt disposal of bankrupt corporations will need to be urgently dealt with.

To solve these problems, we believe that we should play a balanced game between supply and demand and that issues related to the amount and the structure should be given attention. As for structural reform, efficiency improvement, and demand expansion, all three need to be addressed. Excessive cutting of invalid supply without expanding valid supply is likely to result in serious deflation and spiraling economic decline. Demand structure transformation could become a trend thanks to the rise in per capita income. It is thus vital to boost investment, breed innovative production capacity, and expand valid supply while at the same time eliminating the outdated, excessive, and invalid production capacity. To achieve a spirally positive cycle between demand and supply, we need to expand demand by expanding the investment for valid supply so that "innovation would boost growth and demand stabilize employment." In terms of supply, we need to not only reduce invalid supply by reforming the supply structure but also amplify valid supply according to changes of demand objects and structures while also improving quality and efficiency, together with the flexible adaption of the supply structure to the demand structure. In terms of demand, we will need to raise residents' income and expand consumption demand by adjusting income distribution. In the meantime, we should take advantage of interest rate marketization to make sure extensive credit resources allocation meets the demand of private investment so as to promote structural adjustment through effective investment.

Chapter 2
Forecast of China's Economy During 2016–2017

2.1 Assumptions of Exogenous Variables

2.1.1 Economic Growth Rates of the US and the Eurozone

In 2016, the huge volatility in the international financial market, the Eurozone and Japan's negative interest rates policy, as well as the expectation of China's economic slowdown led to a huge increase in the uncertainty about US economic growth. This is likely to slow the pace of interest rate increases in the US and inhibit the appreciation of the dollar, and also make predicting the US economy extremely difficult. According to the latest IMF forecast (January 19, 2016), the rate of US economic growth in 2016 and 2017 will grow by 2.6 %, 0.2 percentage points lower than the IMF prediction in October 2015. Although the easing financial conditions and the decreasing international oil prices will have a positive impact on the economic growth in the euro area through the consumption channel, the risk to Greece's and other Eurozone members' economic growth cannot be ignored. According to the latest IMF prediction, the Eurozone will grow by 1.7 % in 2016, 0.1 percentage points higher than the forecast in October 2015. Economic growth in 2017 is expected to continue at 1.7 % (see Fig. 2.1).

2.1.2 Major Exchange Rates

The People's Bank of China launched a reform of the central parity exchange rate quotation of their currency against the dollar on August 11, 2015. It tried to peg the RMB to the China Foreign Exchange Trade System (CFETS) index and tie it to a basket of currencies (a total of 13). At the end of 2015, influenced by the interest

© Springer Science+Business Media Singapore 2016
Center for Macroeconomic Research of Xiamen University, *China's Macroeconomic Outlook*, Current Chinese Economic Report Series, DOI 10.1007/978-981-10-2068-1_2

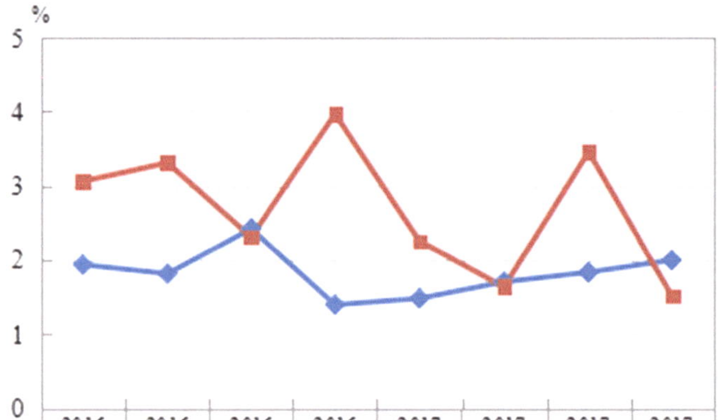

	2016 Q1	2016 Q2	2016 Q3	2016 Q4	2017 Q1	2017 Q2	2017 Q3	2017 Q4
EAGDP_C	1.93	1.81	2.42	1.39	1.48	1.70	1.83	2.00
USGDP_C	3.06	3.31	2.31	3.96	2.26	1.63	3.45	1.51

Fig. 2.1 Assumptions of growth in the USA and the Eurozone (Note: EAGDP_C denotes growth in the Eurozone, while USGDP_C denotes growth in the USA)

rates increases form the Fed and its expectations, as well as the depreciation expectation for the RMB due to China's economic slowdown, the RMB devalued sharply against the dollar, and the pressure on capital outflows increased. At the end of 2015, the central parity exchange rate was 6.4936 yuan to the dollar, indicating an RMB depreciation of 6.0 % compared with that at the end of the previous year. It is expected that the central parity will present violent fluctuations in 2016 and will fall to 6.7 yuan to the dollar by year's end. In 2017, it will remain stable and maintain at 6.8 yuan to the dollar until the end of the year.

The exchange rate of the euro against the dollar will be influenced by the European central bank's monetary policy, the future pace of interest increases form the Fed, and the comprehensive economic situation in Europe and America. On the one hand, since the end of October 2015, the determination of the European central bank to boost the euro zone's economy through a weak euro became increasingly apparent, and it is still possible to ease deflationary pressures through further easing in the future. On the other hand, interest rates will be incrementally increased from the Fed. Influenced by combinations of these factors, the euro is expected to maintain its weakening trend in 2015 and fall against the dollar to \$1.06 by the end of 2016. In 2017, the formation of the Eurozone recovery period will weaken the motivation for European central bank easing; the euro is expected to rebound and perhaps increase against the dollar to \$1.15 by the end of 2017 (see Fig. 2.2).

Fig. 2.2 Assumptions of major exchange rates (Note: ER_W denotes the exchange rate of the RMB against the USD, and USDEURO denotes the exchange rate of the USD against the euro)

2.1.3 The Growth Rate of Broad Money Supply (M2)

In 2015, the central bank cut the requirement reserve ratio (RRR) and lowered key interest rates five times, playing an important role in the "steady growth." The economy still faces downward pressure due to an investment slowdown in 2016, and the CPI is likely substantially lower than the inflation target of 3 %. In this condition, it is expected that the central bank will remain a moderately loose monetary policy to change market expectations, reverse the pessimism, and break the vicious "debt–deflation" cycle. Meanwhile, monetary policy also needs to match the proactive fiscal policy to respond to the central policy tone that both the supply and demand sides should be paid close attention. The Central Bank of China is expected to lower its interest rate by 25 basis points in the second quarter of 2016 and may cut the requirement reserve ratio (RRR) three times in 2016, each time by 50 basis points. The annual M2 growth rate in 2016 is expected to be 13.4 %, slightly higher than the 13.1 % of annual growth in 2017 (see Fig. 2.3).

2.2 Forecasts of China's Major Macroeconomic Indicators for 2016–2017

2.2.1 Forecast of GDP Growth

Assuming the above exogenous variables, the predictions based on CQMM show that, in 2016, China's GDP growth rate will be 6.66 %, 0.25 percentage points lower

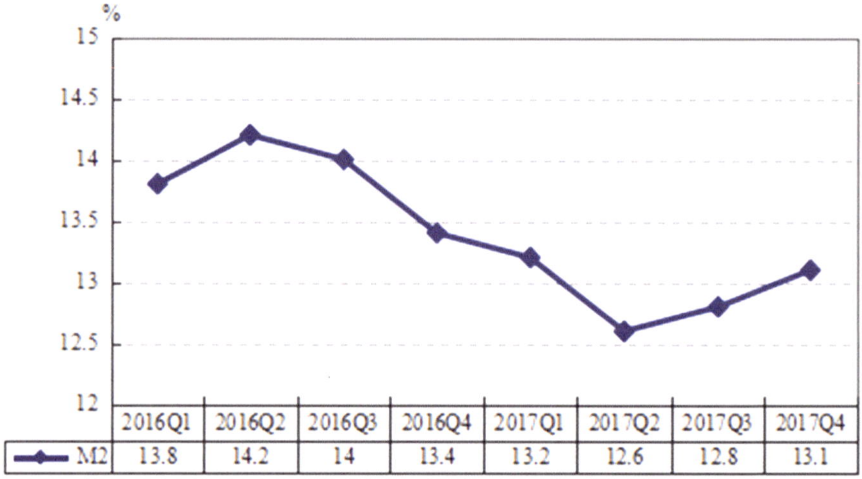

Fig. 2.3 Assumption of the growth rate of M2

than that in 2015. By 2017, the GDP growth rate will be fall further to 6.58 %, 0.08 percentage points lower than that in 2016. This shows that, although China's economic growth over the next 2 years will continue to decline, the decline will slow; economic growth is expected to then gradually stabilize. The downward pressure of the economic slowdown will come from many factors, such as the increase of unemployment, debt risk caused by eliminating invalid capacity, the investment slowdown caused by falling corporate profits and banks' reluctance to lend, and the risk of capital flows caused by RMB exchange rate volatility. On the other hand, the effect of structural adjustment through supply and demand will continue to appear. The continual increase in the tertiary industry's proportion will be beneficial to keeping steady employment. The investment structure adjustment will contribute to improving the efficiency of investment. The transformation and upgrading of the manufacturing industry will be conducive to improving labor productivity and promoting revenue growth. Thus, structural adjustment will gradually become the main force behind stable economic growth.

From the quarterly year-on-year growth rate shown in Fig. 2.4, the slowdown investment caused by cautious bank credit in the process of decreasing production in the first half of 2016 will not be improved. It is expected that GDP growth will continue to slow to 6.61 % in the second quarter. The increasing RMB devaluation expectation will pull export demand, and monetary authorities will implement interest rate cuts at the end of the second quarter to adjust market expectations. In this condition, GDP will grow by 6.68 % year-on-year in the third quarter of 2016 and be back up to 6.70 % in the fourth quarter. Then, because of increasing risk in the international environment, the failure of traditional investment paths, and the cautious attitude of domestic banks to loans, the economy will fall to 6.58 % in the

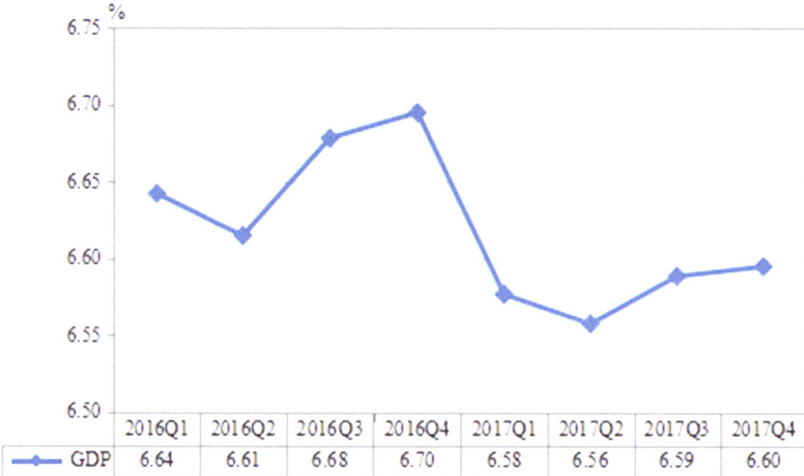

Fig. 2.4 Forecast of GDP growth rate (year-on-year basis)

first quarter of 2017, then continue to dip to 6.56 %. It is predicted that, over the next 2 years, although depreciation will be beneficial for promoting export growth, the high risk in the international environment, the slowdown in investment caused by domestic capital outflows in the capital market, and banks' cautious attitude to loans will still form a strong downward pressure on China's economy.

2.2.2 *Forecasts of Major Price Indices*

The CQMM predicts that the CPI will rise by 1.48 % in 2016, 0.04 percentage points higher than that in 2015. In 2017, the CPI is expected to fall slightly to 1.39 %. By quarters (see Fig. 2.5), influenced by the continued downward economic trend, CPI growth could fall to 1.36 % in the first quarter of 2016, and further fall to 1.27 % in the second quarter and then, under the effect of monetary policy adjustment, rise slightly to 1.6 % in the third quarter and continue to rise to 1.69 % in the fourth quarter. Then, it will fall to 1.62 % by the first quarter of 2017 and fluctuate slightly to 1.43 % in the second quarter to the fourth.

The PPI in the next 2 years will continue to maintain a negative trend, but the decline is expected to gradually narrow in the process of decreasing excess capacity and increasing effective supply. The PPI is expected to be −3.31 % in 2016 and could further narrow to −0.66 % in 2017. The narrowing decline of PPI will be conducive to the restorative growth of the upstream production information corporate profits and reduce business debt burdens. By quarters (see Fig. 2.5), the PPI may fall to −4.2 % in the first quarter of 2016. The index drop is expected to

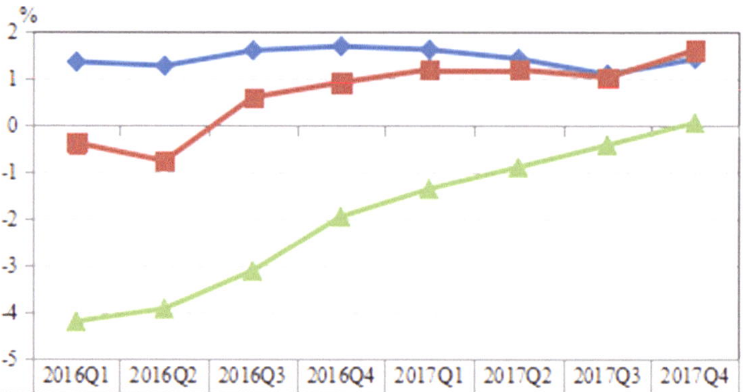

	2016Q1	2016Q2	2016Q3	2016Q4	2017Q1	2017Q2	2017Q3	2017Q4
CPI	1.36	1.27	1.60	1.69	1.62	1.43	1.10	1.43
P_GDP	-0.38	-0.76	0.60	0.92	1.20	1.19	1.03	1.62
PPI	-4.20	-3.92	-3.11	-1.95	-1.36	-0.89	-0.42	0.06

Fig. 2.5 Forecasts of major price indices (year-on-year basis) (Note: CPI, P_GDP, and PPI denotes consumer price index, GDP deflator, and producer price index, respectively)

gradually narrow in the next six quarters and begin to positively grow to 0.06 % in the fourth quarter of 2017, as the external economic environment improves, "One Belt and One Road" construction comprehensively launches, the pressure of eliminating backward production capacity decreases, and the enterprise management situation improves.

In 2016, the GDP deflator (P_GDP) could rise slightly to 0.09 % and further improve to 1.26 % in 2017. It is predicted that, over the next 2 years, the deflation risk to China's economy will be relatively small. By quarters, it could fall to −0.38 % in the first quarter of 2016 and continue to fall to −0.76 % in the second. As a result of the shrinking producer price index decline, the GDP deflator will continue to grow, and its growth rate will increase to 1.62 % in the fourth quarter of 2017 (see Fig. 2.5).

Overall, China's economic growth will continue to decline under the pressure of the investment slowdown over the next 2 years, but the decline will slow. Economic growth is expected to gradually stabilize, and the risk of overall deflation is relatively small. It is expected that the GDP growth rate will be 6.66 % in 2016, 0.25 percentage points lower than that in 2015. The inflation rate will maintain a stable low level, and the CPI will rise to 1.48 %. The PPI is expected to be −3.31 %, and the GDP deflator may be 0.09 %. In 2017, GDP growth may further fall to 6.58 %, but only 0.08 percentage points lower than that in 2016, and economic growth is expected to gradually stabilize. The CPI may rise to 1.39 %, the PPI is expected to be −0.66 %, and the GDP deflator may rise to 1.26 %.

2.2.3 Forecasts of Growth Rates of Other Major Macroeconomic Indicators

2.2.3.1 Export, Import, and Reserve Growth

Although the IMF predicts that global trade in goods and services over the next 2 years will experience restorative growth, uncertainty about the main economic growth and capital market risk remains high. On the other hand, the transformation and upgrading of China's exports are unlikely to be completed in the short term, so export growth will still face strong pressure. The CQMM forecasts that exports in USD at current prices are expected to grow by 0.83 % in 2016, 3.11 percentage points higher than in 2015. Total import growth may fall to −8.36 %, a slight increase of 6.06 percentage points over 2015 (see Table 2.1). By quarters, exports year-on-year in the first quarter of 2016 will continue maintain a negative growth of -1.26 %, recover slightly to 1.33 % in the second quarter, and continue to grow to 2 % in the fourth quarter. Year-on-year growth in imports in the first quarter of 2016 could reach −1.74 %, and then the drop will expand to −13.14 % in the fourth quarter. In 2016, China's net exports as a share of GDP will drop to 1.58 %. There is still the depreciation expectation and pressure on capital outflows due to the economic slowdown. To maintain the stability of the RMB exchange rate, China's foreign exchange reserves will continue to shrink. Foreign exchange reserves are expected to drop to $3.12 trillion in 2016.

In 2017, as external market demand gradually recovers, China's exports will show a resumption of growth. Export growth in USD at current prices is expected to reach 3.08 %. Meanwhile, import growth is expected to be −4.88 %, and the decline will be significantly narrowed. The foreign exchange reserve is likely to remain stable in 2017 and fall slightly to $3.05 trillion (see Fig. 2.6).

2.2.3.2 The Growth Rate of Total Fixed Assets

The excess capacity in manufacturing, the excessive inventory of the real estate industry, and the debt burdens of corporations will continue to put downward pressure on investment. The CQMM predicts (see Fig. 2.7) that, in 2016, the urban fixed asset investment growth rate at current prices is expected to be 9.13 %, 1.11 percentage points lower than that in 2015. In 2017, as the effective investment demand caused by supply and demand structure adjustment will support investment in fixed assets, the urban fixed assets investment growth rate is expected to rebound to 9.22 %, 0.09 percentage points higher than that in 2016. By quarters, the urban fixed-asset investment growth rate (at current prices) in the third quarter of 2016 will peak to 9.62 %. In 2017, it will continue the trend of 2016, falling after rising and then peak at 9.79 % in the third quarter.

Table 2.1 Forecast of growth rates of exports and imports and proportion of net exports accounted for GDP in 2016–2017 (%)

Period	Exports (%)				Imports (%)				The proportion of net exports accounted for GDP (%)
	At constant price	At current price	General trade at current price	Processing trade at current price	At constant price	At current price	General trade at current price	Processing trade at current price	
2016 年	**7.14**	**0.83**	**−0.52**	**1.48**	**2.95**	**−8.36**	**−11.68**	**4.92**	**1.58**
Q1	3.37	−1.26	−3.20	0.57	12.45	−1.74	−6.02	5.72	1.59
Q2	7.65	1.33	−0.14	1.91	5.41	−8.22	−11.49	4.37	1.70
Q3	8.51	1.31	0.97	0.74	0.91	−10.03	−13.60	6.72	1.91
Q4	9.08	2.00	0.42	2.74	−5.50	−13.14	−15.60	2.95	1.10
2017 年	**4.42**	**3.08**	**3.05**	**2.28**	**−1.85**	**−4.88**	**−7.25**	**0.11**	**1.92**
Q1	4.61	1.82	1.16	1.62	−2.82	−7.59	−10.73	−0.67	2.02
Q2	5.00	3.13	3.09	2.34	−1.88	−5.66	−8.37	0.13	2.09
Q3	4.88	4.27	4.68	3.08	−1.22	−3.66	−5.94	0.98	2.23
Q4	3.21	3.08	3.27	2.09	−1.49	−2.38	−3.52	−0.01	1.36

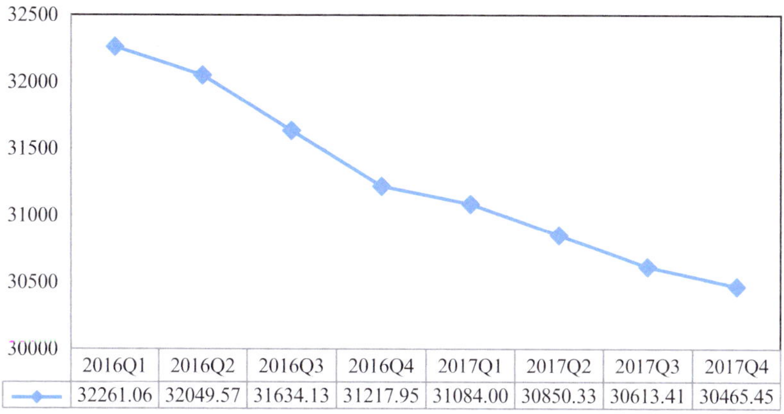

Fig. 2.6 The growth rate of foreign exchange reserves (year-on-year basis)

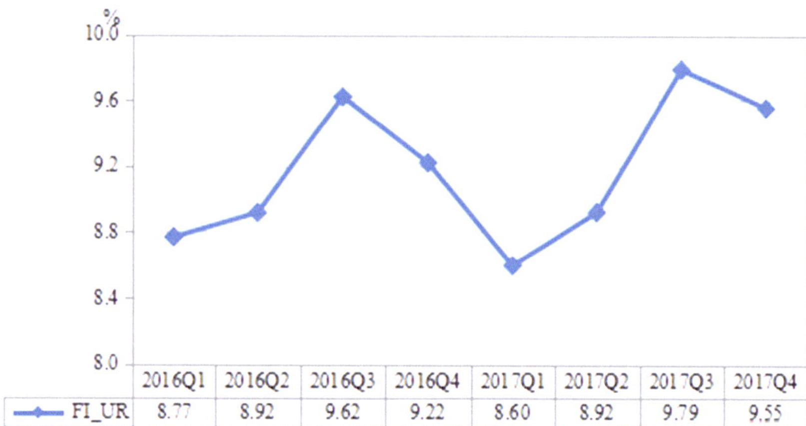

Fig. 2.7 The growth rate of total fixed capital formation (year-on-year basis) (Note: FI_UR denotes the growth rate of urban fixed capital formation at current prices)

In terms of investment resources in fixed assets (see Table 2.2), the fixed asset investment growth from the budget in 2016 is expected to remain at 20.24 % and will fall to 15.73 % in 2017. In 2016, fixed assets investment growth rate from domestic loans will go back up to 0.06 % and then rise further to 2.45 % in 2017. In 2016, the self-financed fixed asset investment growth rate could reach 8.87 % and rise to 9.91 % in 2017. The fixed assets investment growth from other parts in 2016 is expected to rise to 16.64 % and fall to 13.37 % in 2017. Overall, the total fixed asset investment growth rate will remain at 9.54 % in 2016 and at 9.85 % in 2017.

Table 2.2 China's fixed asset investment growth forecasts of 2016–2017

Period	The total fixed asset investment growth	The budget part of the fixed asset investment	Domestic lending part of the fixed asset investment	The self-financed part of the fixed asset investment	The other part of the fixed asset investment
2016	**9.54**	**20.24**	**0.06**	**8.87**	**16.64**
Q1	9.58	19.03	−2.66	8.31	19.17
Q2	9.49	26.95	−0.47	8.69	17.84
Q3	9.34	19.19	1.17	9.17	14.91
Q4	9.73	16.42	2.21	9.27	15.02
2017	**9.85**	**15.73**	**2.45**	**9.91**	**13.37**
Q1	9.79	15.44	1.71	9.87	13.97
Q2	9.66	13.17	1.64	9.99	13.32
Q3	9.98	16.78	3.06	10.05	12.84
Q4	9.95	17.42	3.34	9.75	13.39

2.2.3.3 The Growth Rate of Consumption

In the short term, the growth rate of residential real income is unlikely to increase significantly. Therefore, residential consumption will continue to maintain its current slow growth over the next 2 years. According to the CQMM prediction, in 2016, with the prices kept constant, total consumption will grow by 7.98 %, a decrease of 1.3 percentage points over the previous year. It will continue to fall to 7.32 % in 2017, staying generally stable. In 2016, at present prices, the total retail sales of social consumer goods will grow by 11.53 %, a slight increase of 0.33 percentage points over the previous year, and fall slightly to 10.48 % in 2017.

By quarters, total consumption growth in 2016 (at constant price) will maintain the 2015 trend, falling to 6.74 % in the third quarter, the lowest level of the year. It will continue to decline slowly in 2017 and fall to the annual minimum of 6.59 % in the fourth quarter. The total retail sales of social consumer goods (at constant prices) will keep steady growth in 2016, falling to 6.14 % in the fourth quarter under the base effect of the same period last year. In 2017, it will keep steady, with a slight decrease, and remain between 7.58 % and 13.56 % each quarter (see Fig. 2.8).

Overall, the CQMM predicts that China's economic growth will continue to fall under the pressure of declining investment over the next 2 years, but this decline will slow. Economic growth is expected to gradually stabilize, and the risk of deflation is relatively small.

1. The GDP growth rate is expected to be 6.66 % in 2016 and continue to fall by 0.25 percentage points as in 2015. The CPI will rise by 1.48 %, 0.04 percentage points higher than that in 2015. The PPI is expected to be −3.31 %, 1.9 percentage points lower than that in 2015. The GDP deflator growth rate is expected to be 0.09 %, 0.51 percentage points higher than that in 2015.

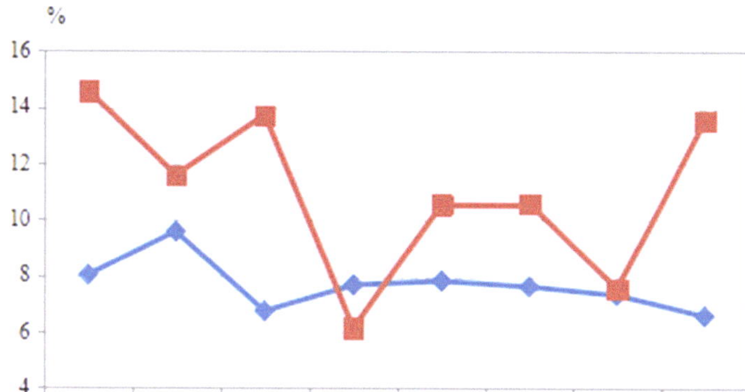

	2016Q 1	2016Q 2	2016Q 3	2016Q 4	2017Q 1	2017Q 2	2017Q 3	2017Q 4
CON_D_C	8.01	9.57	6.74	7.67	7.81	7.62	7.33	6.59
RETAIL	14.59	11.58	13.73	6.14	10.55	10.59	7.58	13.56

Fig. 2.8 The growth rate of consumption (year-on-year basis) (Note: CON_D_C denotes the growth rate of resident consumption at constant price and Retail denotes the growth rate of retail consumer goods sales at current prices)

2. The excess capacity in manufacturing, the excess inventory of real estate, and corporate debt burdens will continue to put downward pressure on investment. In 2016, the urban fixed asset investment growth rate at current prices is expected to be 9.13 %, 1.11 percentage points lower than that in 2015.
3. In the short term, the growth rate of residential real income is unlikely to increase significantly. Residential consumption habits and propensity are even more unlikely to change greatly. Therefore, residential consumption will continue to maintain its current slow growth over the next 2 years. In 2016, the growth rate of social retail sales at current prices will be 11.53 %, a slight increase of 0.33 percentage points over the previous year.
4. Although the IMF predicts that global trade in goods and services will recover its growth over the next 2 years, the economic growth of major economies is still highly uncertain. China's total exports in USD at current prices are expected to grow by 0.83 %, an increase of 3.11 percentage points over that of 2015. The growth rate of total imports may fall to −8.36 %, a slight increase of 6.06 percentage points over 2015.
5. In 2016, a depreciation expectation and the pressure of capital outflow will continue, caused by the economic slowdown. China's foreign exchange reserves will continue to shrink to maintain the stability of the RMB exchange rate. In 2016, foreign exchange reserves are expected to drop to $3.12 trillion.

Chapter 3
Policy Simulation

3.1 Background Analysis of Policy Simulations

Since the People's Bank of China announced the implementation of a managed floating exchange rate regime based on market supply and demand in July 2005, not only the CNY (RMB) to USD exchange rate but also the nominal (real) effective exchange rates started a long process of appreciation. On August 11, 2015, the People's Bank of China launched a reform of the formation mechanism of the RMB central parity rate against the USD. The CNY (RMB) to USD exchange rate ended its unilateral appreciation trend and entered into the stage of volatile fluctuation. In 2015, the RMB central parity against the USD devalued by about 6 %. In 2016, the devaluation trends of the CNY (RMB) against the USD have not weakened and remain volatile and downward.

China's economic growth slowdown and the expectation of an appreciation of the dollar were the main reasons for the rapid devaluation of the CNY (RMB) against the dollar at the end of 2015. The substantial devaluation of the CNY (RMB) against the USD and the continual strengthening of the depreciation expectation exacerbated the tendency of capital outflows. To maintain the relative stability of the RMB exchange rate, foreign exchange reserves rapidly declined. The cumulative foreign exchange reserve decreased by 512.66 billion dollars in 2015, the greatest annual drop ever recorded. The year-end balance of foreign exchange reserves is 3.33 trillion dollars. Given this situation, some have proposed maintaining the currency's decline and adjusting the currency appropriately since, if the currency devaluation is around 13 % until the end of 2016, it will benefit the recovery of manufacturing and boost weak exports. In terms of policy, it will reduce the cost of intervention and the loss of reserves, thus offering a solution for the current predicament.

Is the rapid depreciation of the RMB to the target level helpful in defusing the current exchange rate policy dilemma and mitigating the potential slowdown in economic growth? In theory, this will help strengthen the price competitiveness of

© Springer Science+Business Media Singapore 2016

Center for Macroeconomic Research of Xiamen University, *China's Macroeconomic Outlook*, Current Chinese Economic Report Series, DOI 10.1007/978-981-10-2068-1_3

China's products in the international market and boost weak exports, while turning demand for foreign goods to demand for domestic goods and thus reduce imports. The two effects would work together and expand net exports, with a positive impact on the slowdown in economic growth. On the other hand, the devaluation of the currency will inevitably cause an outflow of capital, with negative impacts on economic liquidity and money tensions. Considering that the foreign reserve plays an important role in current economic liquidity, the outflows will increase the tension on funds and be a drag on future investments. In addition, enterprises still holding more USD liabilities will suffer losses, which may influence their future investments.

Thus, positive and negative effects are intertwined, and the specific comprehensive effects are not easy to identify.

To measure the possible combined effects of the sudden devaluation of the CNY (RMB) accurately, the research team uses a CQMM model to simulate this scenario, quantitatively analyzes the effects of the rapid depreciation of the exchange rate on the economy, and further analyze the combined effects in order to provide references for the formulation of policy.

3.2 Scenario Design of Policy Simulations

Since the Fed raised interest rates on December 17, 2015, currencies in emerging markets devalued competitively; the CNY (RMB) was included in the queue. The devaluation of the CNY (RMB) seems to have become the industry consensus. The debate mainly concerns how and to what extent the CNY (RMB) will depreciate. Most predict that the CNY (RMB) will steadily depreciate by 5 %, and by no more than 10 %, in the coming year. Those who propose that the CNY (RMB) should rapidly depreciate to the target level think that the RMB's exchange rate has been significantly overestimated. They argue that it should depreciate by 13 %, which would help release policy pressure and provide macroeconomic stability. Considering that this forecast has assumed that the RMB's central parity rate against the USD over the next 2 years will gradually depreciate to 6.8 and that the depreciation range will about 5 %, which can represent the former case, the simulation will mainly consider the economic effect of the latter case. Specifically, assuming that the RMB's central parity against the USD in 2016 depreciates by 13 % to 7.3 %, it will further overshoot to 7.45 in 2017 due to the inherent inertia of the depreciation expectation (see Fig. 3.1).[1] By simulating different macroeconomic changes in

[1]Compared to the faster depreciation, the one-time depreciation has greater impacts on the market. The endpoint of depreciation is difficult to determine. The failure experience of the one-time depreciation of the Thai baht during the 1997 Asian financial crisis shows that the so-called "position" in "depreciation to position"is difficult to grasp in practice. Once a currency enters a steep depreciative path, it is likely to arouse excessive nervousness in the market, triggering a self-realizing depreciation expectation "avalanche" and eventually making the exchange rate out of

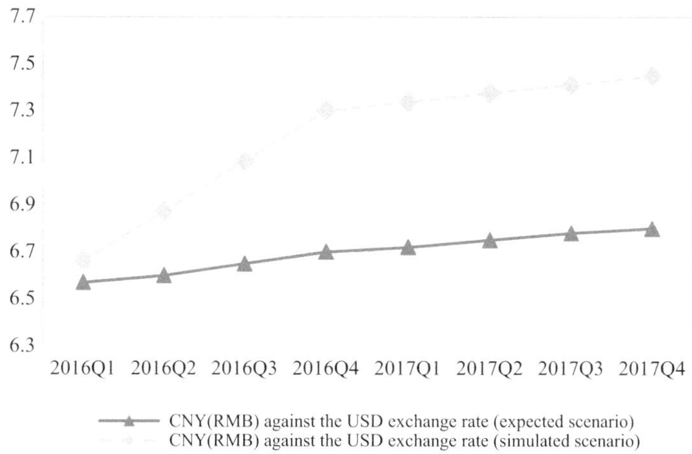

Fig. 3.1 Simulation of exchange rate scenarios (Data source: calculated by research group)

different exchange rate realization paths, we analyze the composite economic impacts caused by the "intervention" policy and the "laissez-faire" policy.

3.3 The Result of Policy Simulations

3.3.1 Impacts of Rapid RMB Depreciation on Imports and Exports

The rapid depreciation of the RMB has an intuitional effect on imports and exports: exports rise while imports decline (see Table 3.1). The growth rate of exports based on current prices and USD rises to 2.67 % in 2016, which is 1.84 percentage points higher than the baseline forecast, and rises further to 4.46 % in 2017, 1.38 percentage points higher than the baseline forecast. In 2016 and 2017, the growth rate of imports reaches −9.45 % and −5.87 % respectively, a decrease of 1.09 and 0.99 percentage points compared with the baseline forecast. Import and export growth rates, which were measured at constant RMB prices, are higher than the baseline forecast, caused by the substantial depreciation of the RMB. If we observe the proportion of net exports of GDP, we find an increase when comparing the net export proportion with the baseline forecast. The result of the policy simulation shows that, if the RMB depreciates rapidly in the next 2 years, it will have obvious effects on export promotion and the improvement of the goods trade surplus.

control and bringing great volatility risks to the macro economy. Therefore, the research team believes that a one-time depreciation is not a policy option. Moreover, technically, this trend is difficult to determine, and it cannot be simulated.

Table 3.1 Imports and exports growth rate simulation on the scenario of RMB depreciation

	Exports(%)				Imports(%)					
	Constant RMB prices		Current USD prices		Constant RMB prices		Current USD prices		The proportion of net exports on GDP(%)	
Period	Forecast	Simulation	Forecast	Simulation	Forecast	Simulation	Forecast	Simulation	Forecast	Simulation
2016	**7.14**	**14.94**	**0.83**	**2.67**	**2.95**	**7.02**	**−8.36**	**−9.45**	**1.58**	**1.83**
Q1	3.37	5.31	−1.26	−0.78	12.45	13.66	−1.74	−2.04	1.59	1.65
Q2	7.65	13.73	1.33	2.79	5.41	8.76	−8.22	−9.08	1.70	1.89
Q3	8.51	18.26	1.31	3.61	0.91	5.90	−10.03	−11.40	1.91	2.23
Q4	9.08	22.49	2.00	5.13	−5.50	0.82	−13.14	−14.95	1.10	1.54
2017	**4.42**	**9.82**	**3.08**	**4.46**	**−1.85**	**0.93**	**−4.88**	**−5.87**	**1.92**	**2.38**
Q1	4.61	15.64	1.82	4.51	−2.82	2.71	−7.59	−9.32	2.02	2.46
Q2	5.00	12.02	3.13	4.88	−1.88	1.58	−5.66	−6.90	2.09	2.54
Q3	4.88	8.57	4.27	5.21	−1.22	0.62	−3.66	−4.34	2.23	2.70
Q4	3.21	3.98	3.08	3.28	−1.49	−1.12	−2.38	−2.56	1.36	1.83

Data source: calculated by research group

3.3.2 *Impacts of Rapid RMB Depreciation on Investment*

Although the rapid depreciation of the RMB can bring export improvements, it could also worsen capital outflow. Simulations based on the CQMM show that, if the RMB quickly depreciates to 1 US dollar for 7.3 yuan in 2016, it will cause the fall of 1.156 trillion-dollar foreign exchange reserves. Since foreign exchange occupies an important share of base currency issue, outflows of this size will inevitably cause a shortage of liquidity supply, which will inhibit investment, already on a declining trend.[2] According to the simulation, social fixed assets investment growth falls from 9.13 % in the baseline projections to 8.02 % in 2016, further falling from the baseline forecast of 9.22 to 7.72 % in 2017 (see Fig. 3.2). This change will also cause the share of investment out of GDP to fall from 45.99 % and 45.14 % to 45.67 % and 44.65 % in the next 2 years.

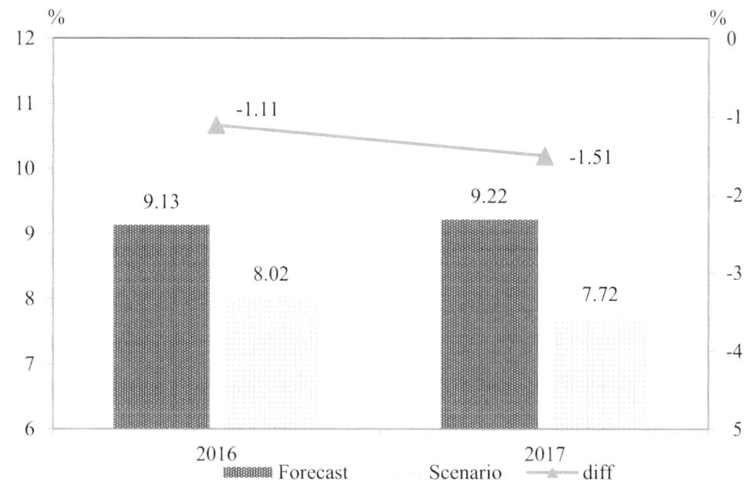

Fig. 3.2 Changes in social fixed assets investment growth rate (Source: calculated by Research Group. Note: Forecast represents benchmark forecast; Scenario is the simulation results; diff is the difference between scenario and baseline forecast)

[2]While the Central Bank can supplement market liquidity using monetary policy tools such as the SLO, SLF, MLF, and PSL (established in 2013) and traditional means such as reducing the reserve rate, the scenario of rapid depreciation, which will only make the situation worse and strengthen the expectation of RMB depreciation, will accelerate currency depreciation.

3.3.3 *Impacts of Rapid Depreciation of RMB on GDP Growth*

The depreciation of the RMB has positive impacts on imports and exports and negative impacts on investment; the two impacts work together. GDP will both grow and decline during the forecast period (see Fig. 3.3). In 2016, spurred by the abrupt depreciation of the RMB, investment contraction caused by substantial capital outflows exceeds the impact of net export growth, and GDP growth falls from the anticipated level of 6.66 to 6.45 %, declining by 0.21 percentage points overall. In 2017, with the weak depreciation expectation and eased capital outflows, GDP growth will slightly increase from the expected level of 6.58 to 6.59 %. However, if we deduct the base effect, the overall net growth effect is not very positive.

To sum up, if we let the RMB depreciate quickly to the target level (i.e., depreciate 13 % until the end of 2016), it may help increase net exports, which will have a positive impact on the overall economy. However, the large-scale capital outflows caused by this rapid depreciation would put pressure on already declining investments, which would have a greater negative impact on the overall economy. Thus, the consequences of indulging a depreciation policy may do more harm than good.

This analysis does not take into account the possible adverse effects of RMB depreciation on the external environment. As the world's second-largest economy, China's exchange rate policy is important. If we allow the RMB to depreciate rapidly, external economies will inevitably make targeted responses, which will greatly change the external environment negatively. First, even if assuming that the RMB will depreciate more than 10 % is reasonable in the current market expectations, indulging depreciation would be bad for the guidance and management of

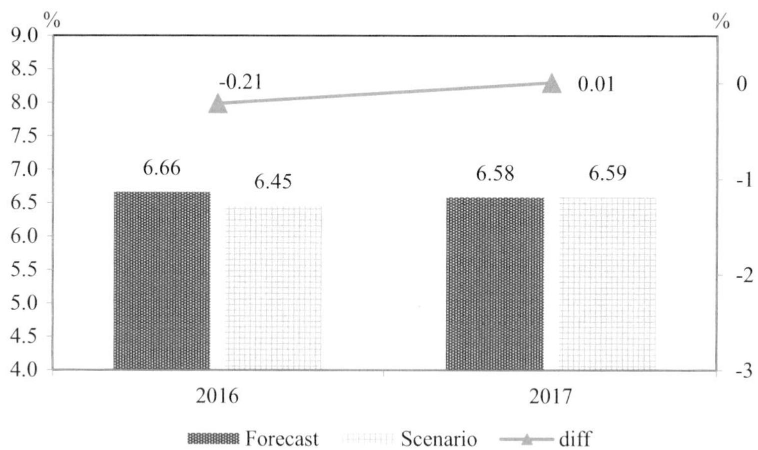

Fig. 3.3 The growth rate change of the total retail sales (Source: calculated by Research Group. Note: Forecast represents benchmark forecast; Scenario is the simulation results; diff is the difference between scenario and baseline forecast)

market expectations. However, an indulged rapid depreciation may also cause depreciation expectations to form into a self-reinforcing cycle and push depreciation completely out of hand. Speculative capital will add fuel to the fire and make it uncontrollable.[3] The cost of the Central Bank's exchange rates intervention will decrease at low currency levels, but, once the market loses confidence in the Central Bank, it will increase the difficulty of intervention. Second, large-scale RMB depreciation could trigger competitive currency depreciation in other countries, especially emerging-market countries, which will undermine the effect of export promotion and make the depreciation endpoint even more difficult to control. Third, rapid RMB depreciation and a potential "depreciation war" will lead to massive capital outflow from emerging markets, worsen the external economic environment, and damage the recovery prospects of external demand, while making it difficult to achieve the desired level of export boost. Finally, since the depreciation may cause economic risks and shocks, making this choice would damage China's international image, the image of the RMB as an international currency, and the Central Bank's policy credibility; these potential losses are immeasurable.

In addition, large-scale depreciation would have negative structural impacts on domestic economic conditions. First, during past currency appreciation periods, the corporate sector accumulated much USD debt, and rapid depreciation will place additional burdens on these enterprises. Second, boosting exports through the exchange rate can help inefficient enterprises survive, temporarily relieving local pressure, but this is not conducive to eliminating backwards production capacity, and will create hidden problems for supply-side reforms. Conversely, the advantage of maintaining the stability of the RMB is that, first, it will help the RMB play a better role as the international currency following the One Belt and One Road strategy, facilitating foreign investments; second, currency stability will help firms address the cost pressures and competition they are facing, thereby stimulating the optimal allocation of factors, foster the survival of the fittest, promote mergers and reorganization, and improve enterprise efficiency; third, currency depreciation can boost exports, partly by offsetting the rising costs of labor and wages, and will make export enterprises return to the old ways whereby there is only low value-added and labor-intensive product competition, as maintaining currency stability ensures the relative attractiveness of native wages, increases the human capital of the export sector, and improves productivity.

Therefore, we believe that maintaining the stability of the RMB in the current economic environment is the better policy choice.[4]

---

[3]In the 1997 Asian financial crisis, Thailand ended its baht intervention, and the baht depreciated 18 % that day, achieving the expected depreciation (20 %). However, the baht continued to fall 60 %, greatly exceeding the expected depreciation.

[4]Although the Central Bank might intend to use this opportunity to increase the RMB fluctuation range, the one-way fluctuation expectation is quite strong. Given the current economic environment, the research group believes that it is not a good time to take this action.

Chapter 4
Supply Structure Reform Under Demand Structure Transformation

4.1 Background Analysis

To cope with the 2008 international financial crisis, China's government has implemented the enormous fiscal stimulus policy represented by the "Four Trillion" investment plan; however, after only 2 years, China's ascending economic growth rate took a turn downward again and kept descending until the present. This cruel reality has urged policymakers to fully reflect on the defect of the "broad irrigation" macro-control policy, which depends mainly on the gross demand and demand side, and consider the fact that no breakthrough has been made with the long-term devotion to the transformation of economic development patterns. China's government proposed the new policy of structural reform of the supply side by the end of 2015 to adapt to the economic "new normal," improve the effective supply ability, and upgrade the quality of economic growth. They also established the five main tasks of "de-capacity, de-stock, de-leverage, reducing costs, and filling the gaps" as well as the overall macro-control policy of the "stability of macro policies, the precision of industrial policies, the flexibility of micro policies, the concreteness of reform policies, and the fundamentality of social policies." China has firmly determined the strategic direction of starting from the supply side, stabilizing economic growth, and fully developing China's tremendous economic potential and is fully prepared to make an "addition, subtraction, multiplication, or division" during industrial structure adjustment, accelerate the transformation of economic development patterns, and cultivate to form new economic growth impetus.

The new policy of supply side structural reform is a further exploration and refining of the judgment by the current government based on "dealing simultaneously with the slowdown in economic growth, making difficult structural adjustments, absorbing the effects of the previous economic stimulus policies" and the "new normal" in terms of China's economic growth in the past few years; it is also

© Springer Science+Business Media Singapore 2016
Center for Macroeconomic Research of Xiamen University, *China's Macroeconomic Outlook*, Current Chinese Economic Report Series, DOI 10.1007/978-981-10-2068-1_4

the governance strategy proposed by the top decision makers based on a comprehensive and deep realization of the current economic situation, targeting the structural, systematic and essential problems within the economic reality. China has an expansive internal market and is smoothly stepping over the poverty growth stage with the help of the external market and industrialization. The key elements that have sustained China's economic growth have been transferred to internal China; what constraints China's economic development now is the structural and systematic contradiction of its unbalanced development instead of aperiodic and external shocks. The coexistence of excessive production capacity and insufficient effective supply are typical characteristic of China's current economy.

However, how to carry on with supply side structural reform requires further investigation. The crucial questions are, first, what is the background of the current economic development stage in which severe excessive production capacity and insufficient effective supply coexist? Second, is it the "invisible hand" or the "visible hand" that can effectively accomplish the supply side structural adjustment? Finally, how can the "invisible hand" perform in the accomplishment of supply side structural adjustment?

We believe that the key for smoothly carrying out supply side structural reform is to clearly identify the demand structure and its fundamental development and variation trends. By adapting to the demand structure transformation in the transition period from the above average-income stage to the advanced-economy stage, addressing the systematic and policy-related barriers in terms of timely adjustment when the supply structure cannot fit the demand structure transformation, the market mechanism can accomplish supply structure adjustment faster, better, and more thoroughly than the "visible hand".

First, in the past two decades, as China smoothly upgraded from a low-income country to an above average-income economic entity, the residents' consumption structure has witnessed dramatic changes. The ratio of food, clothes, and household equipment in terms of consumption expenses has decreased sharply, and the proportion of heavy consumption expenses such as housing and transportation has increased rapidly. From 1992 to 2014, the proportion of food, clothes, and household equipment expenses out of urban residents' total expenses decreased about 31.0 percentage points, while the ratio of housing, transportation, and communication increased by about 27.1 percentage points. Correspondingly, China has gradually formed an investment structure with the real estate and transportation industries as its core. In terms of the 2014 fixed assets investments, the proportions of the real estate, automobile manufacturing, railway, shipping, and other transportation equipment manufacturing industries out of total investment is about 27.3 %; when taking matched road transportation and railway transportation into account, the ratio increases to 33.7 % and surpasses the contemporary fixed assets investment ratio of the manufacturing industry overall (33.3 %).

However, amid its economic growth, China has gradually entered into a transition period from the above average-income stage to the advanced-economy stage. China's consumption structure has given signs of a new round of upgrade and transformation. The consumption structure, consisting mainly of substance consumption such as housing, transportation, food, and clothes, has gradually transformed into a consumption structure that attaches equal importance to service consumption and substance consumption. In 2014, the proportion of urban residents' food, clothes, and household equipment expenses was about 44.37 %; housing, transportation, and communication expenses totaled about 35.69 %, the two ratios dropping 0.27 and 0.11 percentage points, respectively, from 2013; medical care, education, culture, entertainment and other goods and services expenses totaled about 19.94 %, 0.38 percentage points higher than in 2013. According to the transformation and upgrade experience of advanced countries, new demand is likely to soon replace the housing and transportation consumption demand that has increased rapidly for nearly two decades and become the new increased consumption demand impetus of China's economy for the next 10–20 years. However, contradicting the trend in which the residents' consumption structure is quietly upgrading, the investment structure does not show any corresponding structural changes. In the tertiary industry, the proportion of fixed assets investment in the education and health industry dropped from 3.05 % and 0.71 % in 2004 to 1.24 % and 0.60 % in 2013 respectively, lagging far behind the investment in the real estate and transportation industries; investment in the culture, sports and entertainment industry was only 1.12 % in 2013.

The contradiction in the investment and consumption demand structures leads to the coexistence of excessive production capacity and insufficient supply. On one hand, from 1999 to 2015, the annual average growth rate of products inventory for all industrial sectors was as high as 12.1 %. The upstream and downstream industries closely linked with the real estate and transportation industries, such as the nonferrous metal smelting and rolling processing industry (16.3 %), ferrous metals smelting and rolling processing industry (13.7 %), ferrous metals mining and dressing industry (22.6 %), coal mining and washing industry (17.2 %), and the furniture manufacturing industry (15.0 %), as well as some industries less correlated with the real estate and transportation industries but with strong industrial competition, such as the food manufacturing industry (13.0 %), textile, clothing, shoes and hats manufacturing industry (14.0 %), agricultural and sideline food processing industry (15.9 %), and the timber processing, bamboo, cane, palm fiber and straw products industry (15.9 %), all have higher annual inventory growth rates. On the other hand, modern service products, especially healthcare and education products related with residents' consumption upgrade direction in the transition period, are severely insufficient. In 2014, the ratio of teachers to students in primary and secondary schools and the number of hospitals and sickbeds per 10,000 people was 0.066, 0.189, and 36.27, respectively, about 1.67, 1.96, and 3.17 times the 1978 figures, but real GDP per capita was as high as 19.78 times the 1978 total. The difficulties of enrolling in primary and secondary schools, of being treated in hospitals, and of living after retirement have already became national issues.

Second, taking history as a guide, at the beginning of the 1990s, with residents' consumption expenses gradually being dominated by housing and transportation expenses, China implemented marketization reform for the real estate industry,[1] carried out the "open-door" policy, introduced foreign capital and joint ventures early in the transportation industry (especially in the automobile industry),[2] increased the housing supply capacity tremendously, upgraded automobile and related products, and transitioned residents' consumption demand. China therefore accomplished the optimal allocation and efficient use of resources; this also provided a motivation for China to smoothly step over the poverty trap and upgrade residents' consumption structure and the match with the supply structure. Currently, however, because of the long-term counter-market existence of the education and healthcare industries as institutional organizations, China lacks the adjustment of "invisible hands" and is keen on regulations by "visible hands." On one hand, because of the constrained supply of the monopolized resources, the product supply ability is severely insufficient and the demand exceeds the supply. On the other hand, with the government's price regulation, the price restriction power for monopoly behaviors has been throttled, amplifying demand and worsening the mismatch between demand and supply. Therefore, although a severe excessive production capacity problem exists in China's economy, this does not mean that aggregate demand is insufficient; rather, the supply structure cannot satisfy the changes in the demand structure, largely because of the lag in institutional reform and the severe government monopoly.

Third, we need to fully develop the ability of the "invisible hand" to adjust the supply structure; the job of the next stage needs to address the trend variations of residents' consumption demand structure over the next 5–10 years and 10–20 years

---

[1]In June 1991, the State Council issued *the "inform regarding continue promoting the reform of urban housing system positively and steadily*" and proposed promoting housing system reform in all kinds of ways such as the stepwise raising of rents, the payment of rental deposits, new houses with new institutions, house-building through cooperation and fundraising, and public housing sales. In October, during the second working conference of the national housing system reform, the rent reform principles of "refund for the overpayment and supplement for the deficiency," or no subsidies for small rent increases, were proposed. in November, the General Office of the State Council forwarded the "*suggestions about comprehensively promoting urban housing system reform*" by the leading housing system reform group of the State Council and clarified the guiding ideology and fundamental objectives of housing system reform, signifying that the reform has ended the exploratory and pilot phase and entered a new stage with the comprehensive promotion and integrated matched reform.

[2]In 1983, automobile production companies were allowed to have a certain proportion of self-marketing rights. In January 1984, Beijing Jeep automobile Ltd., jointly operated by a Beijing automobile manufacturing factory and the American automobile company, was established. In May of the same year, the state-operated Changan machinery factory and Japan Suzuki automobile industry Ltd. signed a technology introduction agreement in the form of combined technology and trade to produce the ST90 series minicar. In November, a Shanghai tractor automobile company and the Thailand Zhengda Group Hong Kong Yichu Investment Ltd established the Shanghai Yichu Motor Ltd. In May 1996, the Sino-German joint venture Union Automobile Electronics Ltd was founded in Shanghai Pudong New Area. In March 1997, the Sino-American joint venture Shanghai General Motors Ltd. and Pan-Asia Automobile Technology Center Ltd. signed a joint venture contract. In April 1998, Guangzhou and Japan Honda signed a joint venture contract. The opening of the automobile industry occurred exceptionally smoothly.

with the help of institutional reform, mechanism innovation, market opening and related policies, and the elimination of outdated production capacities. We should build products and a modern service supply system that can satisfy the new consumption structure, form effective supply, and reshape the new impetus for economic growth. This is not only beneficial to the addition and multiplication in the supply side structural reform, further clarifying the emphasis and direction of supply side structural adjustment with concrete targets and pertinence, but can also prevent the circular appearance of the excessive production capacity problems at the same time, fostering an adaptation between the newly formed supply ability and consumption demand and realizing a benign industry evolution process, during which new supply creates new demand, new demand promotes new consumption, and new consumption forces back the creative destruction produced by the new industry. The crucial points of supply side structural reform are relaxing regulations, releasing the energy supply, providing a broader platform for the invisible hand of the market, and boosting investment efficiency.

4.2 Evolution and Trend Prospect of China's Urban and Rural Residential Consumption Structure

4.2.1 Evolution of Urban and Rural Residential Consumption Structure

Using the questionnaire data about eight kinds of consumption expenses per capita for urban and rural residents from 1992 to 2012, we can depict the variation trends in China's consumption structure for the two decades. First, the proportion of food expenses has narrowed substantially. In 1992, among all kinds of expenses for urban residents, the food expense covers 52.9 %; until 2012, the food expense covers only 36.2 %, which has decreased 16.7 percentage points and about 0.8 percentage points annually (see Fig. 4.1). In the same period, the proportion of rural residents' food expenses falls more steeply, decreasing from 57.5 % in 1992 to 39.3 % in 2012 (see Fig. 4.2). After adjusting the statistical caliber for expenses, the proportion of urban and rural residents' food expenses in 2013 and 2014 decrease further: the proportion of urban residents' food expenses decreased to 30.1 % and 30.0 % respectively, and the proportion for rural residents decreased to 34.1 % and 33.6 % respectively.

Second, the proportion of clothing, household equipment, and service expenses is stable but with a decreasing trend. The two kinds of expenses for urban residents kept decreasing in the first 10 years; a recovery appeared in around 2004, but the rate basically maintained stable. In 2012, the clothing expenses and household equipment and service expenses of urban residents totaled about 10.9 % and 6.7 % respectively, decreasing 3.2 and 1.7 percentage points, respectively, from 1992 (see Fig. 4.1). The proportions of the two kinds of expenses for rural residents

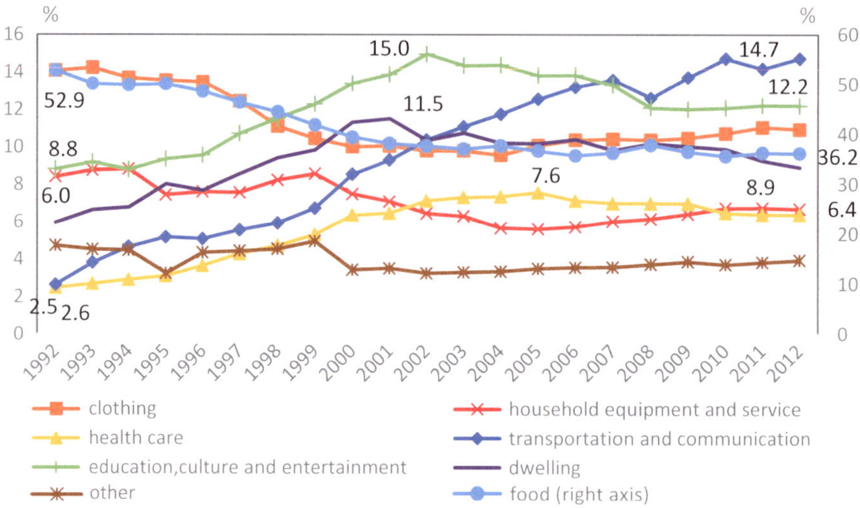

Fig. 4.1 The proportion changes of eight kinds of consumption expenditures of China urban residents (Data source: from CEIC database)

showed smaller changes; from 1992 to 2012, the proportion of clothing expenses changed from only 8.0 to 6.7 %, while the proportion of household equipment and service expenses increased slightly from 5.6 to 5.8 % (see Fig. 4.2).

Third, transportation/communication and residence expenditures increase significantly. For urban residents, the proportion of the two kinds of expenses surpassed food expenses, totaling around 1/3 of all expenses. For the transportation/communication expenses, the proportions for both urban and rural residents presented an increasing trend. The proportion for urban residents increased quickly from 2.6 % in 1992 to 14.7 % in 2012 (see Fig. 4.1); for rural residents, the proportion increased from 1.9 % in 1992 to 11.0 % in 2012 (see Fig. 4.2). After the uniform urban and rural household survey and the adjustment of related statistical caliber in 2013, the proportion of residence expenditure jumped to 23.3 % and became the second-largest expense after food expenses. In 2014, it dropped slightly back to 22.5 %; the proportion of rural residence expenditure increased from 18.4 % in 2012 to 21.1 % in 2013.

Fourth, education, culture, and entertainment expenditures display an "increase first and decrease after" trend. The turning point in urban residents' education, culture and entertainment expenditures appeared in 2002: after achieving its highest proportion of 15 %, it fell gradually and kept steady at around 12.2 % for several years. The highest proportion for rural residents, of 12.1 %, appeared in 2003, and the proportion gradually decreased afterwards. In 2012, it went back to 7.5 %, which was almost its level in the beginning of the 1990s. After the adjustment of the statistical caliber of 2013, the proportion increased to 10.1 % but remains relatively low.

Fifth, an urban-rural disparity appeared in health care expenditures. Urban residents' health care expenditures increased continuously from 1992 for the next

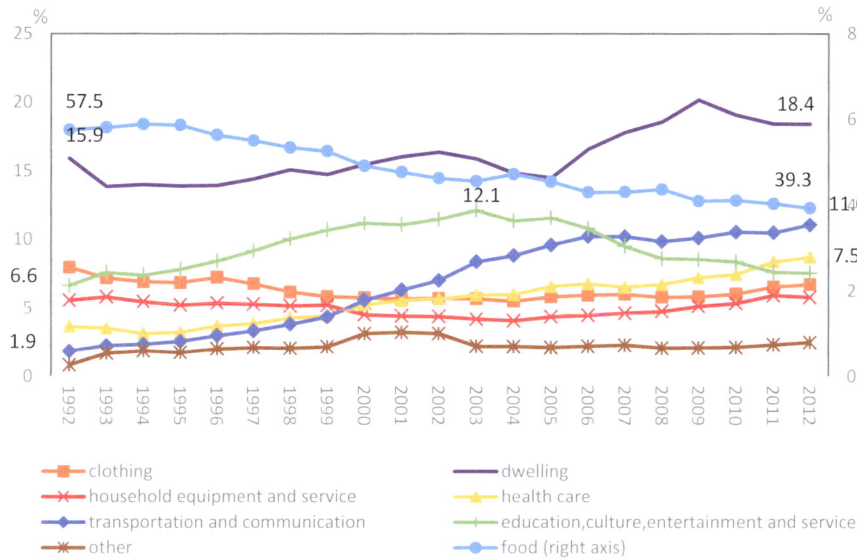

Fig. 4.2 The proportion changes of eight kinds of consumption expenditures of China rural residents (Data source: from CEIC database)

13 years and then decreased gradually from 2006 to 2012; it still has a decreasing trend. After the adjustment of the statistical caliber of 2013, it fell further to 6.1 %. Rural residents' healthcare expenditure has maintained an increasing trend, going up all the way from 3.7 % in 1992 to 7.5 %, more than doubling. The trend differences between them were likely related to the differences in the healthcare system after 2005. The medical security enjoyed by urban residents was better than that of rural residents, causing the slow growth in the healthcare expenditures of urban residents.

To briefly summarize, in the past two decades, as China's economy successfully passed through the poverty barriers, Chinese consumption behaviors have had two main features.

First, the proportion of food and clothing expenditures out of total expenditures decreased substantially, declining gradually from over 70 % to below 50 %. Meanwhile, transportation/communication and residence expenditures greatly increased, gradually becoming more important consumption expenses. This consumption structure evolution generally occurred according to the theoretical expectations of development economics and was also consistent with prior international development experiences. When a country transitions from the poverty stage to the middle-income stage, accumulating capital and wealth, consumers will gradually reduce their consumption of items needed for fundamental survival such as food and clothing and gradually increase their higher-level substance consumption. This is the demand-side explanation for the high-speed growth of China's automobile and real estate industries over the past two decades: amid the strong Chinese demand for transportation and housing, once the institutional barriers that constrained the supply of the two products were broken, the two industries developed and quickly became pillar industries supporting economic growth.

Second, the proportion of education/culture/entertainment, healthcare, and other service products has been relatively low, representing less than 20 % of total expenses. In addition, the proportion of the two kinds of expenses has shown a decreasing trend since 2002 because, first, of the squeeze from the increase in China's main consumption items such as housing and transportation/communication and, second, of the supply system obstruction caused by these service products and their rising prices.

4.2.2 Trend Prospects

Starting from the current consumption structure, how will the Chinese consumption structure evolve over the next 5–20 years? Theoretically, amid the transition of the country from an above average-income entity to an advanced-economy entity, residents' consumption structure will begin to transform from a structure dominated by materials consumption to a structure that gives equal priority to service consumption and high-quality materials consumption, but it will gradually tend to rely on service consumption. Given the transformation and development experiences of South Korea, this judgment is basically reliable.

In 2014, the three kinds of urban expenses (education/culture/entertainment, healthcare, and other items) accounted for about 19.9 % of total consumption, approximately equal to the level in South Korea at the beginning of the 1980s (18.8 %). China's 2014 real GDP per capita based on 2005 prices, 3862.0 dollars, was basically equal to South Korea's real GDP per capita in 1981 (4151.2 dollars). After 1981, South Korea's real GDP per capita increased to 8158.1 dollars within 8 years, turning it into an advanced economic entity. As it stepped over the middle-income trap, South Korea's expenses for education, health, culture/entertainment, and miscellaneous increased swiftly from 18.8 % in 1981 to 28.6 % in 1989, and then further to 33.8 % in 2009 (see Fig. 4.3). South Korea's economic development and structural transformation track indicate that, as China's economy gradually transforms from above average-income to advanced-income over the next 5–20 years, Chinese education, culture/entertainment, and healthcare expenditures will greatly increase.

In addition, as South Korea transitioned from an above average-income to an advanced-economy entity, amid the changes in all classes of consumption expenditure from the 1970s onwards, the rapid growth of education, culture/entertainment, healthcare, housing, transportation, and communication industry expenditures helped them to surpass food and clothing expenditures by the beginning of the 1990s. Initially, housing, transportation, and communication expenditures increased more quickly, but since 1998, after the expenses' proportions had increased for 23 years, the proportions of housing, transportation, and

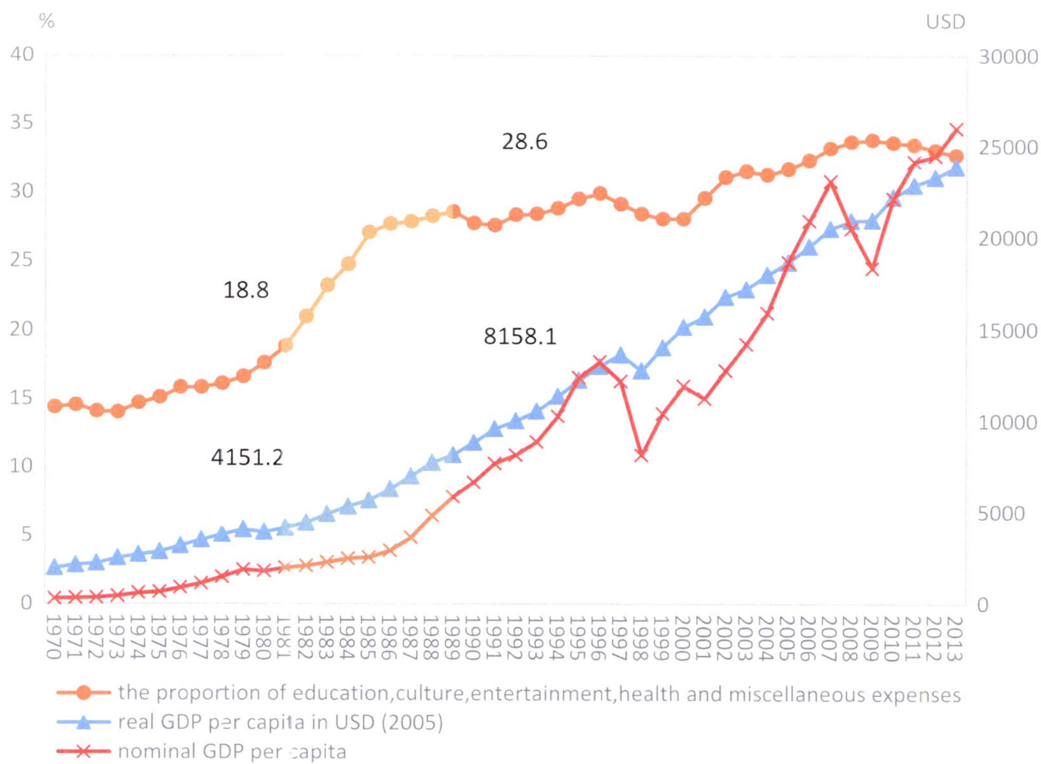

Fig. 4.3 The comparison of real GDP per capita(the right axis) and residents expenditure proportion of service products such as education, culture and entertainment(the right axis) (Note: The service procucts such as residents education include the summation of education, health, culture-entertainment and miscellaneous expenditures, the data is from NDATA;the data of nominal GDP per capita calculated in dollar and real GDP per capita (deflated by the price in 2005) are from CEIC database)

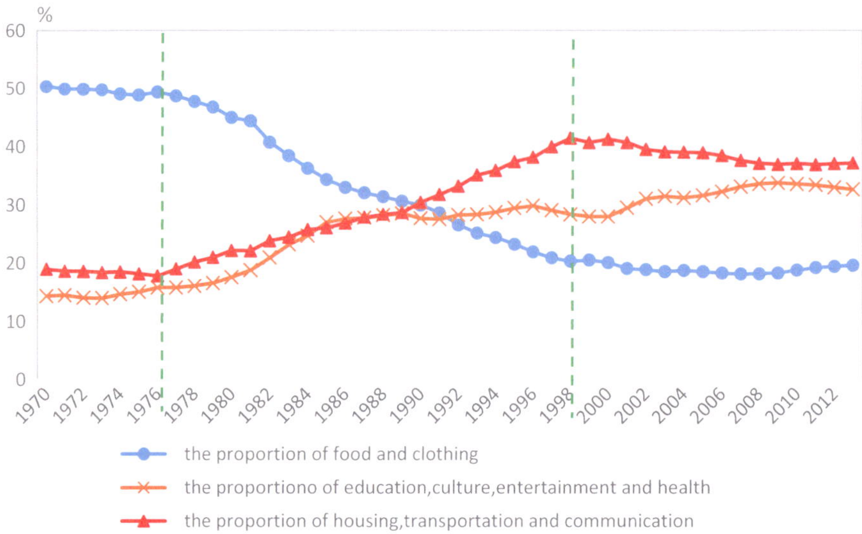

Fig. 4.4 The change of classified expenditure proportion of residents' consumption in the South Korea (Note: UNDATA divides the consumption into 12 categories: 1. food and beverage; 2. alcohol, tobacco, narcotic; 3. clothing, shoes; 4. housing, water and electricity, fuel; 5. furniture and house maintenance; 6. health; 7. transportation; 8. communication; 9. culture and entertainment; 10. education; 11. catering and lodging; 12. sundry. The expenditures of education, culture, entertainment and health include the items of 6, 9, 10 and 12; The food and clothing expenditures include the items of 1 and 3; The expenditures of housing, transportation and communication include the items of 4, 5, 7 and 8. The data is from UNDATA)

communication expenditures started to decrease; this trend continued until the present. However, the proportions of education, culture/entertainment, and healthcare have kept increasing, and the gap between them is narrowing quickly (see Fig. 4.4).

Therefore, the research team believes that, within the next 10 years, as China transitions from an above average-income economic entity to a high-income economic entity (when nominal GDP per capita during the 13th Five-year Plan will exceed 10,000 dollars), China's consumption structure will undergo a new round of upgrade and transformation; the structure previously dominated by materials consumption such as housing, transportation, food, and clothing will gradually give equal priority to service consumption and high-quality materials consumption, and the latter will gradually replace housing and transportation consumption demand, which has enjoyed rapid growth for almost two decades, and become the new main consumption demand impetus for China's economy over the next 10–20 years.

In fact, after the rapid growth of the last 30 years, the developed region on the eastern coast has already reached, or has almost reached, the level of high-income countries; the residents' consumption capacity and **concept** have also changed. Of material product consumption, the proportions of housing and automobile consumption have increased substantially; service consumption demand, including more health and convenient life, higher education, entertainment/culture, and sports products, has expanded accordingly, triggering rapid growth in the fitness, entertainment, tourist, intelligent device, Internet, and information industries. The Chinese have increasingly high expectations of product quality. Comments on online shopping websites such as Taobao used to concentrate on cheap prices, but they are starting to focus on such issues as product quality and whether the products are fake. Most overseas purchases used to be for luxury items, but they are gradually expanding to daily necessities, illustrating that income increases are pushing domestic consumption preferences towards those of developed countries and that product quality expectations are also increasing.

In contrast to the upgrading trend in China's consumption structure, however, the production capacity for most material products is excessive or even severely excessive, especially for general consumer goods, export-oriented labor intensive products, and real estate (stimulated by the housing consumption of the last 20 years), as well as the upstream industries that provides services for those sectors.

If we observe this issue from the perspective of economic development leading to the transformation of the demand structure, we not only need de-stocking for these industries but we must also embark on de-capacity. As with the demand structure transformation, demand in these industries will inevitably shrink; it is impossible to count on a spring coming for those who survive that harsh winter.

Take real estate as an example. In 2012, the dwelling area per capita of urban Chinese was 32.9 square meters,[3] approximately equal to levels in developed countries such as the UK, France, Germany, and Japan at the beginning of the 1990s.[4] Room for growth is limited. Demand for real estate has likely hit a peak: (1) the rigid demand among the house-purchasing population born during the third baby boom (1983–1990) is weakening; (2) when urbanization exceeds 50 %, expansion will slow. Therefore, the real estate absorption capacity of the "new urban citizens" is decreasing. The rising stocks in the real estate market, the reversal of the supply and demand structure, and the weakened expansion expectations of the real estate industry for future demand will cause firms' investment passion to decline significantly. In 2015, total investment in China's real estate development was about 9.60 trillion RMB, an increase of only 1 % over 2014. It is predicted that investments in real estate development will decrease in 2016. Finally, from the longer-term perspectives, prior international experience indicates that, as a country gradually moves from the middle-income stage to the higher-income stage, the nation's consumption structure, which depended on heavy consumption such as housing consumption and automobile consumption, is gradually replaced by the consumption of modern service products (Zhou 2014). This means that, if China

[3]Jiabao Wen, *The Government Working Report*, the National People's Congress, March 5, 2013.

[4]The literature we use to arrive at our conclusions includes the following: Bai, X. and Wang, H. W., "The Synthesized Measurement Study of the Housing Industry: Based on the Engel Coefficient and the Analysis of Dwelling Area Per Capita Model", *Journal of Finance and Economics*, 9, 2005; Guan, K et al. *Modern Housing Economy*, China Architecture and Building Press, 2002, p. 3 (quoted).

can smoothly step over the GDP per capita barrier of 10,000 dollars in the next 5 years, housing consumption demand will weaken. In other words, even though powerful policies can stimulate the smooth working of de-stocking in the real estate industry, this will probably happen merely through the early increase of demand in the next several years, when real estate will no longer act as an important pillar industry.

The general consumption products and export-oriented labor intensive industries and the upstream industries that provide services to them also face severe de-capacity. If we conduct only de-stocking, de-leverage, and de-capacity, the economy will decline spirally. When subtracting, it is important to also perform addition. In the background of demand structure transformation, it is crucial for supply side structural reform to increase the effective production capacity and open up new investment areas according to the development and variation trends of the demand structure.

China's consumption structure is transforming from a stage dominated by material consumption to a stage that gives equal priority to service consumption and high-quality material consumption, but will gradually depend on service consumption. In addition, the manufacturing industry shows a severe excess of general production capacity; however, China's tertiary industry, especially the modern service industry, still faces a severely insufficient effective supply ability because of institutional barriers.[5] This asymmetry in the supply and demand structure significantly restrains the satisfaction of Chinese consumption demand and the improvement of the consumption rate. However, the main causes of the deficient effective supply ability and the low efficiency of the modern service industry are the lagging institutional reform, the severe government monopoly, and excessive state ownership in the economy. Take the industry-classified employment numbers and proportion of fixed asset investments as an example. In 2014, among the industry-classified employees of urban units, the employees of state-owned units in the manufacturing industry totaled only 4.0 %, but the employees of state-owned units in the tertiary industry totaled 59.7 % (after deducting the wholesale–retail, lodging and catering, public administration, social security, and social organization industries). The proportions of employees of state-owned units in the education/health, social work, and culture/sports/entertainment industries was as high as 92.8 %, 86.9 %, and 73.1 % respectively; among the industry-classified fixed asset investments (excluding peasant households), the proportion of state-controlled investment in the manufacturing industry was only 8.3 %, while the proportion of state-controlled investment in the tertiary industry was about 45.2 % (after deducting the wholesale–retail, lodging and catering, public administration, social security, and social organization industries). The proportion of state-controlled investment in the education and health, social work, and culture and sports industries (excluding entertainment) was as high as 72.1 %, 66.3 %, and

[5]Of course, parts of the manufacturing industry also show an insufficiency of effective supply, but we do not analyze them deeply here.

50.8 % respectively. Therefore, we are not breaking away from consumption when we emphasize the adjustment of the supply structure. On the contrary, the supply adjustment in the next phase should involve the upgrading and transformation of consumption demand. With the help of institutional reform, mechanism innovation, market opening, and related policies, we should make use of the invisible hand of the market, remove outdated production capacity, build products and a modern service supply system that can satisfy the new consumption structure, form effective supply, and reshape the new impetus for economic growth. The key for supply side structural reform is relaxing regulations, releasing energy, leaving more space for the market, reducing institutional transaction costs, increasing the quality and efficiency of the supply system, and improving investment efficiency.

To verify their conclusions, the research team builds a dynamic general equilibrium model for the production and consumption of two goods. Assume there are two kinds of consumer goods, C_{1t} and C_{2t} in this economy, and the corresponding production factories, Y_{1t} and Y_{2t}. C_{1t} represents material goods; their production is under perfect competition; C_{2t} denotes service products, and their production is under perfect monopoly because of institutional restrictions. The greatest difference between perfect competition and monopoly is that the former involves a price taker, whereby the producer does not have the ability to adjust prices and therefore realizes profit maximization mainly through production adjustment; in the latter, the producer can not only choose to adjust prices but can also realize profit maximization via production adjustment. To restrict the price adjustment ability of monopoly producers, we assume a cost of price adjustment. The representative resident will choose the best combination of consumer goods through the maximization of the utility function, and the producers will start production according to this best combination of consumer goods, thus matching the consumption structure and production structure. Additionally, to show the supply distortion in the service product sector caused by the monopoly, the research team also examines the service product sector operating under perfect competition and compares this situation to the basic situation.[6]

The results of the model are as follows.

First, in the stable situation, if the consumption weight of the material goods is greater in the representative household, the factor productivity is higher in the material sector, and the price adjustment cost is higher in the service sector, leading to a greater production of material goods and a lower production of service goods out of total production. We can also conclude that, when the consumption structure inclines to service products, the price adjustment costs of service product producers and the reversed change of factor productivity will probably hamper the effects of the resource optimization and allocation that the consumption structure upgrade of material consumption should bring to service consumption and therefore distort the consumption demand and supply structures, lowering the efficiency of factor allocation.

[6]The model building and deduction are presented in the appendix.

Second, after breaking the monopoly in the service products sector, in the steady situation, the production of service products will increase; moreover, the supply structure of the material products sector and service products sector will change along with the changes in the representative household's consumption structure.

Third, when the service sector products become more important to the representative household, a production structure leaning more towards material products is likely to bring more distortion to resource and factor allocation, further lowering the supply efficiency of the corresponding production.

In a word, when the service sector is under monopoly, even though the material producers can satisfy the changes in material consumption, the service producers probably cannot catch up with the changes of consumption structure in a timely way because of the lag in resource adjustment and cost adjustment problems such as supply restraint, thus lowering the production of service products, increasing prices, and promoting higher material consumption because of the decrease in the relative price. Finally, the lagged adjustment of the production structure can cause the non-optimization of resources and factors, leading to price distortion; on the other hand, it can also hamper consumption structure transformation and cause consumption to change according to production, decreasing residents' total utility level.

Chapter 5
Policy Implications and Suggestions

From the above analysis, our research team proposes the following policy suggestions.

1. The government should pay close attention to the current economic slowdown, which is posing huge risks to China's economy.

First, under the huge pressure of the global economic downturn, China's economic structural adjustment began to slow in 2015. Although the tertiary industry's share of GDP in China exceeded 50 % in terms of industrial structure in 2015, this was still relatively low compared with the average level (55 %) of other countries with similar per capita GDP. What's more, current labor productivity in the tertiary industry is low. Deregulation and liberalization in the modern service industry have been seriously delayed. This not only reduces production efficiency and economic growth but also directly inhibits the speed of the increase in residential income, which is not conducive to the rapid expansion of the tertiary industry. Second, in terms of investment structure, in 2015, under the loose monetary policy, the growth rate of private investment dropped sharply, and the pace of the improvement in the investment structure slowed. Thus, the loose monetary policy did not allocate credit resources effectively to the real economy to meet the needs of private investment. Meanwhile, there remain tangible and intangible obstacles to and restrictions on private investment. Third, in terms of the manufacturing industry structure, the expansion in the manufacturing sectors slowed, but the structure is upgrading slowly. Growth rates in some manufacturing industries have declined, such as in general equipment manufacturing, special equipment manufacturing, railway, shipbuilding, aerospace and other transportation equipment manufacturing, as well as computers, communications, and other electronic equipment manufacturing.

Second, the continued economic slowdown has pushed the depreciation expectation into a self-reinforcing cycle. After the People's Bank of China launched the reform to improve the middle price quotation of the RMB exchange rate mechanism on August 11, 2015, the RMB depreciated sharply against the dollar. Although the current account maintains a surplus, the pressure of capital outflows is

© Springer Science+Business Media Singapore 2016

Center for Macroeconomic Research of Xiamen University, *China's Macroeconomic Outlook*, Current Chinese Economic Report Series, DOI 10.1007/978-981-10-2068-1_5

increasing constantly due to the superposition of factors such as shrinkage in the actual use of foreign capital scale, the expansion in China's foreign investments, expectations of a further interest rate increase from the Federal Reserve, and RMB depreciation expectations resulting from the domestic economic slowdown.

Finally, the economic slowdown and intensified structural deflation have increased the risk of a debt crisis. Structural deflation is the result of massive production capacity stimulation to tackle the financial crisis (including the expansion of the real estate industry) since 2012. Efforts to digest the overcapacity are struggling, however, for institutional reasons, thereby increasing structural deflation. As excess capacity is digested, it is important to solve the problems of the reemployment of the unemployed and the debts of bankrupt enterprises.

2. Supply-side structural reform should take demand structure transformation as a guideline for the new stage of development. While reducing supply in some areas, the government should increase supply in others, expand demand, and ensure its steady growth.

After the per capita GDP exceeded $5000 in 2010, China's economy entered a new development stage, as China transitions from an upper-middle-income to a high-income economy. China's macroeconomic policy pays close attention to the international financial crisis, a cyclical impact coming from outside, ignoring the structural and institutional adjustments caused by the transformations of this new development stage. The government focused excessively on expanding aggregate demand, thus covering up and even intensifying the structural contradiction between supply and demand. It also delayed the urgently needed structural adjustment and institutional reform in the development stage transformation, leading to the current serious excess capacity, insufficient effective supply, and downward economic growth.

However, the internal requirement generated by the change of economic development stage is irresistible, as is reflected in the differences between the growth rates of the manufacturing and service industries during the continued economic slowdown. China will face the transition from an upper-middle-income to a high-income economy. In this new development stage, the government should conduct supply-side reform, reducing supply in some areas while increasing it in others to adapt to the demand structure transformation trend, which will achieve supply-side structural adjustment faster. Increasing effective supply and adjusting the supply structure will effectively expand domestic demand, realize a positive economic operation cycle, and stabilize economic growth.

3. The government should take the supply-side structural adjustment as a direction, enlarge investment, ensure steady growth, and adjust the structure with new capacity.

Weak demand is the main reason for the current economic slowdown. In 2015, the PPI price dropped to a record level of $-5.2\,\%$. In this condition, simply removing capacity will lead to the superposition of falling demand, a higher debt crisis risk, and a downward economic spiral. It is necessary to increase investment, expand demand, and utilize the excess capacity to stabilize economic growth. Increasing investment is also essential with a negative investment price. Although aiming to expand current demand, investments must focus on the future and take the supply-side structural adjustment as a direction according to the demand transformation trajectories. Therefore, while accelerating the removal of excess capacity and inventory, the government should build emerging industries, break through system bottlenecks, and seek to lengthen the short stave of supply through a long-term view and consumer demand structure trends over the next 5 to 10 or 10–20 years.

Over the next 10 years, the residential consumption structure will undergo a new round of upgrading with the transition from an upper-middle-income to a high-income economy (China's per capita nominal GDP will exceed $10,000 during the period of the 13th Five-year Plan). Residential consumption mainly comprises physical consumption such as housing, transportation, food and clothing, but it will gradually transform into a new consumption structure featuring service consumption and high-quality physical consumption. The proportions of expenditures on education, culture/entertainment, and healthcare will increase significantly and become a driving force for consumer demand over the next 10–20 years. In response to the improvement of the consumption structure, the government must improve the gravely insufficient effective supply capacity of modern service products as soon as possible.

Compared with developed economies, China suffers from a serious shortage of basic infrastructure per capita or per unit of land area in both urban and rural areas. It also lags behind developed economies' levels of disaster preparedness and mitigation, with huge gaps between regions. This hinders economic exchanges between regions and the equalization of economic development and public services. Investment demand in this field is quite strong.

4. The government should "vacate the cage to change the bird," meaning that it should obtain investment funds through investment substitution.

Due to the continued economic downturn, governmental income growth at all levels dropped sharply. In 2015, public finance income grew by 8.4 %, a decrease of 0.2 percentage points over the previous year. Fiscal expenditures rose by 15.8 %, an increase of 7.6 percentage points over the previous year. Fiscal deficits totaled 2.3551 trillion yuan, accounting for 3.5 % of GDP. Because of the indebtedness of governments at all levels, it is worth considering the sources of the money used when the government expands investment in infrastructure.

The investment growth rate of the private economy declined in 2015. The loose monetary policy did not allocate credit resources to the real economy, especially the private sector, effectively. The limited investment field is another important reason for the slow growth.

Therefore, investment substitution and implementing mixed ownership reform through the transfer of high-quality state-owned shares to attract private investment will help government departments obtain infrastructure investment funds. It will also expand the investment field and the growth rate of the private economy. In addition, the current state-owned economy is concentrated in the modern service industry. As a result, mixed ownership reform in the related state-owned enterprises will break the monopoly, deregulate, and bring in market competition. This will greatly improve the efficiency of resource utilization and production in the modern service industry and ultimately increase supply efficiency.

Investment substitution must be implemented on the premise that state-owned enterprises will lose their controlling status; then, mixed ownership reform should occur in state-owned enterprises to realize market competition.

The government should also reexamine the modern service industry in terms of non-market competition but from a new perspective. Through this new arrangement, departments providing public services and social welfare should be given a chance to enter the market and increase the potential for competitive operation.

5. It is important to stabilize the value of the RMB to create a good external environment for supply-side structural adjustment. The government should maintain the current RMB exchange rate, steadily promote the pace of interest rate liberalization, strengthen policy openness and transparency, and manage market expectations effectively. On the one hand, this will be conducive to strengthening domestic and foreign capital's willingness to invest in China, alleviating the rate of capital outflow, and avoiding the negative impact of the temporary shortage of funds. On the other hand, it will also help stabilize the volatility of the external economy caused by the Fed's raising of interest rates, especially given the continued economic slowdown among emerging and developing countries. It would also be beneficial to implement a new opening strategy such as the One Belt and One Road plan and create a good external environment for the domestic supply-side structural adjustment.

Chapter 6
Comments and Discussions

6.1 Professor Gao, Peiyong, President, National Academy of Economic Strategy, Chinese Academy of Social Sciences

Today, I would like to talk mainly about tax cut. This round of tax cut is entirely different with previous ones in thought, ideology and angle. Therefore, it could not be evaluated under the same system as before.

Firstly, this round puts emphasis on promoting tax cut by the method of reform, which means it has at least two features: it is not only about the implementation of tax policy, but also should be combined with conduct the tax reform. Secondly, we also must include the new concepts, thoughts and strategies about managing state affairs since the third plenary session. Therefore, many operations are quite different with before, such as the relationship between tax and price, and tax cut is always closely related to the relationship between tax and price. The relationship between tax and price in China is quite different with foreign countries. The commodity price is just cost plus profit overseas, but in China, the price includes the tax.

The ultimate goal of this reform is to let the market play the determinant role in the resource allocation. The market means the price. When the price contains too many tax factors, it could not be the one which can completely reflect the resource allocation conditions and guide the optimization of resources allocation. Over 70 % of China's tax could be added into the price, such as turnover tax, value-added tax, business tax, consumption tax, urban construction tax, tariff, etc. The GDP was 67.67 trillion last year and the tax revenue was about 14 trillion, and 70 % of the tax was turnover tax, which was about 9 trillion. We can image, if so many taxes should be integrated into the price, could the price be the signal of precise guidance of the resources allocation? During the structural adjustment and reform, if the price

© Springer Science+Business Media Singapore 2016

Center for Macroeconomic Research of Xiamen University, *China's Macroeconomic Outlook*, Current Chinese Economic Report Series, DOI 10.1007/978-981-10-2068-1_6

couldn't get rid of the tax factors, what could be the results? The structural reform must return to the tax reform, even deducting a little bit turnover tax and indirect tax, it could reduce the disturbance of taxes for the prices.

Secondly, it is about the allocation of the taxes. The efficiency principle of taxes is much more considered since the new China, such as the question that how to guarantee the taxes which required by the exercise of state power entering into the national treasury steadily, timely and fully. We don't care so much about whom on earth pays the taxes. If not focusing on this issue, you have no way to touch the supply-side and also the detail of supply side structural property. For instance, who pays the 14 trillion taxes revenue finally? Are they entrepreneurs or the residents? For the residents, which specific income group do they belong to? For the entrepreneurs, which industry is it? Which round is it during the enterprise operation? We must extend from the total quantity to the structure, once extending, many new issues appeared. The allocation of taxes in China is according to the consumptions actually, who consumes more, and who pays more taxes. Whose consumption ratio in terms of income is higher, who relatively pays more taxes. So, turnover taxes and indirect taxes are digressive taxes. You have to consider this issue when you adjust the supply side structure.

The allocated tax revenue according to the income is much less, only covering from 6 to 7 %. That means, among 14 trillion tax revenue, only 6–7 % is individual income tax, nearly no tax revenue is allocated according to the wealth. Therefore, the redefinition of tax standards involves the internal reform of taxes and we have to consider this issue when talking about reducing taxes this time.

When talking about fiscal policies, we have to discuss the tax policies, and no such discussions can stay away from increasing the deficit and use the major part of deficit to support the tax cut. The finance and taxation department could tell you that the current situation of fiscal income is very severe. Professor Yanwu Wang used official numbers when talking about the fiscal revenue deficit just now, but there are other explanations when publishing these numbers. For example, the growth rate of fiscal revenue was 8.4 % last year, but immediately in the following, the number was 5.9 % using the same statistical caliber. The governmental funds revenue was not included in the fiscal budget before 2014, but now five kinds of funds are transferred into the general budget. The special factors of increasing income still need to be excluded, and if we do so, the growth rate of fiscal revenue really has some problems. Fiscal revenue of central government could even negatively grow. Considering these issues, when we talk about the tax cut and total quantity, we cannot only increase several hundreds of millions deficit. It does need increasing, but after the increase, what can we do for the balance of fiscal revenue and expenditures, and how? We have to consider about this issue. I suggest that when talking about the tax cut, we need to wholly consider the tax cut and other government budget's revenue and expenditures plan. Only looking at the fiscal budget, the ratio of fiscal deficit to GDP is 2.4 %. If we also take the funds budget, the social-security budget and state-owned capital budget, this deficit ratio comes down to only 2.1 %.

Besides, the tax cut must be specific, including the questions on which kinds of taxation and for whom the tax should be reduced. The supply side structural reform emphasizes that we should focus on reducing the corporate income tax, but not the individual income tax. The entrepreneurs pay 90 % of the 14 trillion tax revenue, and if individual business is added, the proportion is around 94 %. The individual income tax only covers about 6 %. We need to classify these 18 kinds of taxes and be sure which kind of tax should be reduced for entrepreneurs. It is important to study which types of tax should be cut and don't take one standard for everything. If we don't study this, the operation of tax cut policy is like stepping on the cotton, we have no confidence at all.

Fourthly, it is the fiscal system. For this fiscal system reform, two signals deserve attention. On one hand, under the background of fully promoting the replacing of business tax with the value-added tax, we need to carry out the interim provisions of rationalizing the income system. The current basic thought is still the method of money distribution system. For instance, after the promotion of replacing the business tax with the value-added tax in May, the tax revenue of 5 trillions is going to be cut. The 5 trillion is the reduced quota of local taxation, through the transfer payment by the central government and it subsidizes the local government through other channels, this is the idea of the money distribution system. Actually before 1994, the fiscal system employed by our government is all about the money distribution system, after the reform, we once carried out the all-around contract system and all they distributed is money. The reform thought after 1994 is the tax distribution system. What do they distribute? It is the source of taxation, for example, the land. People farm their land individually and you can spend all that you harvest. Therefore, in the operation of tax reduction policy, we have to consider the differences of the tax distribution system and the money distribution system. Who should take the responsibility for the tax distribution and tax cut? They are different. On the other hand, during the process of fiscal system reform, the current primary job is the reform of governmental authorities, and this is the main reason that the fiscal system is not rationalized in the last two decades. During this process, the tax cut should focus on the changes of taxation management system between the central government and local government.

In a word, this round of tax cut is not like before. Firstly, the economic backgrounds are different. Secondly, the policy goals are different. So we need to have some new considerations and new thoughts. It has been emphasized that we are referring to the structure transfer when we talk about the demand and referring to structure reform when talking about supply. We cannot only talk about the total quantity and ignore the structure. The structure is the detailed problem and is something that we never cast an eye over before and thought it was insignificant. However, if we don't have the structural analysis as the support, the policy plan in the level of total quantity must be unrealistic.

6.2 Professor Zhang, Liqun, Deputy Director, Department of Macroeconomic Research, Development Research Center of the State Council

The economic situation this year stably moves toward a good direction, and the growth rate will not be lower than last year. The reasons mainly come from two aspects. On the one hand, I think this year is the period when the lasting effects of the previous steady growth appear.

Firstly, it is the steady situation of employment, income and consumption. Their effects have appeared continuously in the several recent years. Even though the growth rate of residents' income and the growth rate of consumption both decrease, compared with the growth of GDP and the growth of industry, their decrease range is the minimum. This situation, I think, will continue to play its role in this year and it is the important variable to postpone the decrease of the economy. Several factors such as the guarantee of the employment, helping the poor and the concern of people's primary livelihood are supporting it. This is a very important element for stabilization.

Secondly, it is the investment of infrastructure. The infrastructure investment covers only 17 % of the total investment in 2012, and this proportion increased to 22 % in 2015. The growth rate of the infrastructure investment is the highest of all kinds of investment. This shows that, from the aspect of stabilizing the growth, the government still uses the method of strengthening investment, but with lower frequency and strength than in the package planned economy. The growth of the infrastructure investment this year will continue to play its role as the investment growth stabilizer.

Thirdly, it is the real estate market. The overall recovery of the sales situation in the real estate market in 2015 is not an accidental phenomenon. It is the reform under the support of multiple factors. (1) Urbanization. The permanent resident population of last year increased about 22 million again, the urbanization ratio changed from 54.77 % in 2014 to 56.1 %, increases by 1.6 percentage points again, This shows that China's urbanization is still under way. This is the basic factor supporting the rigid demand of the urban real estate. (2) The housing price in the metropolis. Its performance is stable in the recent 2 years and this situation plays a very important role in correcting the behavior of waiting for the decrease of housing price to buy with cash in hand in the metropolis. (3) The policy. The policy adjustment of mortgage loan in the recent 2 years has played a vital role in increasing the rigid and improved housing purchasing ability. The combined three factors have supported the recovery of real estate demand.

Of course, the problem of population decline in the middle-sized and small cities needs to be solved. The statistical survey shows that in the second-tier cities such as Xiamen and Suzhou, the increasing speed of urban new population starts to exceed the first-tier cities. The urbanization is still under way, and the supporting power for the real estate market is still effective.

The growth rate of real estate investment will keep decreasing this year. If we plus the housing area under construction with the houses in stock, the digesting time we need now is about 6.5 years. From 2005 to 2015, the average digesting time is 5.15 years for this decade. Therefore, the 6.5 years of 2015 is still higher. The de-stocking is indeed the important task. However, it was 6.9 years in 2014. This year, the growth rate of the construction area, completed area and land-taking area are all shrinking obviously. The sales are increasing. Therefore, the digesting time of inventory is decreasing. It will support the real estate construction this year and at least the recovery will be shown in the first-tier and second-tier cities. With the improvement of the financial situation of real estate developer, the whole building progress under construction will speed up. The capital resource of real estate entrepreneurs last year increased by 2.6 %, and the growth of real estate investment is 1 %. The growth rate of real estate capital resource is higher than the real estate investment, and this is an important symbol predicting the changes of real estate investment trends.

From the view of the whole investment, the infrastructure investment and the real estate investment this year together have presented the trend from decrease to stability. Due to the policy of stabilizing growth from 2012, the effects have already shown in consumption, infrastructure investment and real estate investment. This is also the first kind of reason supporting the economy stability in 2016.

The second kind of reason is the 13th five-year plan. This year is the first year. From the fifth plenary session of the Central Economic Working Conference last year and city working conference, the government has made many strategic plans and deploys. The new policy effects of stabilizing growth have already played their roles this year. The supply side structural reform is from previous extensive, low-level and quantitative expansion to the intensive and quality-beneficial bdevelopment. It involves the survival of the fittest entrepreneurs in the market and the reselection by the market, and the "de-capacity" and "de-leverage" this year will witness the actual effects. The situation of economic operation with illness will be gradually improved, which will support the improvement of survival environ ment of entrepreneurs. The utilization of capacity will gradually increase. This is the beneficial factor for manufacturing investment.

Another factor is the new urbanization. The State Council issued the *several suggestions for promoting the new urbanization construction* in February this year, making several aspects of specific plans for new urbanization. First is to develop the city agglomeration. The joint development of the big, middle-size and small cities will be gradually discussed this year. The project construction of interconnection and intercommunication will start to show its effects, which starts to alleviate the problems of decreasing population in middle-sized and small cities. Secondly, the importance of long-term planning increases and the planning ability improves. The effects of planning on the urban construction start to be reinforced. Thirdly, the function of the urban system, especially the underground infrastructure and public service ability increases, and has attracted more and more concern. Fourthly, it is the increase of urban governance ability. The urbanization is the important factor constraining China's economic development. The new urbanization could play an major role in several aspects such as the development of real estate, manufacturing industry and the increase of labor supply stability.

Therefore, in my opinion, the economic development this year is stable with improvement, and the growth rate will not be lower than last year.

6.3 Professor Zhang, Ping, Deputy Director, Institute of Economics, Chinese Academy of Social Sciences

Before, we used to think that in the catching up process of backward countries, the structural reform is mainly about the issue of dual economic structure, by transferring the traditional agriculture department to the industry department, completing the transformation of modern sectors, and this is also the completion of economic structure transformation. Because all the departments are modern sectors, we can conduct the totaling and clearing. The demand and efficiency could determine the factors flow among the industry structures, and the heterogeneous department features do not exist. However, in 2006, China entered into the middle-income stage, you finally will find that this structural reform doesn't disappear but becomes more, that is, the heterogeneous sectors are not eliminated during the modernization, but instead of them are administrative regulation departments. This is quite different with the equilibrium mode proposed by the developed countries.

The involution of one country's economic structure usually follows three laws, which are the demand, efficiency and the similarity of structure.

Firstly, the demand can lead to the structure reform. The Engel Law says that, with the increase of the income level, the proportion of food consumption over the whole consumption expenditures is lower; if there is further increase in income, the proportion of material consumption over the whole consumption expenditures is lower, and the proportion of service consumption is higher.

Secondly, it is the equilibrium mechanism of department's productivity difference. After all the industrial departments become the modern sectors, the resources between departments flow according to the productivity. Along with the competitions, the industrial structure tends to be steady, the heterogeneity between industrial departments is eliminated, and the structure problem transfers to be the issue of total quantity.

Thirdly, it is the similarity of economic structure. The economic development laws of every country in the world all tend to be the same gradually, and the consumption proportion could increase. Sometimes you can have both the high exportation and investment, but as the economy grows maturity, the whole economic structure will converge to a basic standard structure and then evolve.

After China stepped into the middle-income stage, firstly, the friction between the demand structure and supply structure appears obviously, and this friction is the economic structure servitization, which we mention a lot. China entered into the middle-income stage in around 2006. Even though the tertiary industry didn't exceed the secondary industry until 2013 and didn't reach 50 % until 2015, from 2007, the proportion of tertiary industry has always been increasing. As the proportion of tertiary industry increases, the level of urbanization increases and the consumption contribution rate also keeps growing. This is the essential feature of economic structure servitization.

The economy structuralization is caused by the demand structure, and therefore couldn't be changed by man's will. However, the reform of demand structure did not cause the reform of supply, and this can be seen mainly in two aspects. One is the un-satisfaction, for example, the difficulty of getting medical service and the difficulty of receiving the education. The other is that the labor productivity of China's tertiary industry is of course lower than the manufacturing sector, so the inverse efficiency allocation appears in the resources allocation. The research of its reasons is the key to exploring China's current structure reform.

Through the industrialization and the improvement of industrial departments' proportion, generally, all the developing countries can break the poverty trap. But after the entrance into the middle-income stage and the servitization of economic structure, you will find that regarding the structure, the tertiary industry and consumption proportion of many backward countries are the same as the developed countries. But they may not successfully step over the middle-income stage, and this is quite different with the industrial period. This is one topic I think deserves to be discussed today, but why?

You could find that the high proportion of consumption and service and the high urbanization rate are the main structural features of developed countries. However, you may also find that some other countries, such as many Latin American countries, can also meet this standard, but still couldn't break the middle-income trap. The World Bank does the statistic for 50 years and got to know that only 13 countries have escaped from the middle-income trap among around 100 countries. So we can see that this period seems not like the break of the poverty trap, which has a correct industrial road.

The ratios are similar in many countries, for instance, the urbanization rate is very high in Latin American countries and is even higher than that of developed countries, but they are blamed for the population drift. The Latin American countries also have higher tertiary industry proportion than developed countries do, but there are many informal department employment, and all of them are operated in a low-level tertiary industry. Also, their consumption is high but mainly low-level consumption, which does no good to the human capital improvement. Under this premise, even its consumption, tertiary industry and urbanization are all high, the country finally transfers to the low-efficiency mode and can not witness the real economic innovation and development. Therefore, we can say that, the economic structure servertization is not only simply about the proportion of tertiary industry, urbanization and consumption, but about its content: does the modern service department rise rapidly? Can the departments with large demands like

Science, Culture, Health and Physics be formed? The more important thing behind is that after the consumers enjoy the service brought by the rapid rise of these departments, they can continually increase the human capital by these spiritual consumption and not just about simply eating and drinking. Therefore, the labor force, especially the reproduction of high-quality human capital starts from the consumption, and promotes the supply of modern service industry, thus increase the consumption level of human capital and form the innovation of human capital to create more values, then the new circulation is formed. If it couldn't be improved, the human cannot make the innovation, the modernization of tertiary industry is also hardly completed, so the efficiency increase of tertiary industry is just empty talk. We did the research and found that if we want to step over the middle income trap, all-people innovation can come true only through the human capital increase. We need put more efforts.

Among the group between 20 years old and 34, the popularizing rate of university education should increase to 40 %. Then after 10 years or 15 years, the innovation of this country can have a strong foundation. China needs 10–15 years to reach this education level, and another 10 years later, our innovative departments can finally grow.

Traditionally the consumption was a passive cost item of labor reproduction during the industrialization period, but now it is the precondition for innovation in developed countries, that is, the starting point of human capital reproduction. Is it true that only the people receive the improvement of human capital can make innovations? One of the important logic starting points is consumption. If a country wants to step over the middle-income trap, firstly, the human capital must be improved; secondly, the modern service industry related with the human capital, which is, the Science-Culture-Health-Physics industry with the largest demands, must rise rapidly; thirdly, these two rapidly rise are shown as the increase of innovation contribution, so the contribution rate of TFP should reach the level of 40 % , then you can enter into the orderly growth process.

After China's industrialized structure changes, it soon enters into the economic structure servitization process. Moreover, the servitization process of economic structure is not only simply about the increase of ratios, but more importantly, is about the growth of physical human capital, modern service industry and innovation contribution rate. Without the growth of these three factors, you might drop down to the low-efficiency mode during the economic structure servitization process. We know that the efficiency of many traditional service industries is far less than the manufacturing industry. But the demanding law has determined that when people think the physical goods are excessive and don't need to consume so much, it is evitable that we will enter into the economic structure servitization process, therefore, man's will couldn't change this process.

The contribution of TFP to the growth actually has already decreased by 16 % these years. During the 13th five-year plan, if the ratio cannot reach 30 %, we still need to worry about our economic growth.

Therefore, we need to do better supply-side reform. This supply-side reform can be summarized as: among the current technical departments, can China produce a department of knowledge production and innovation independently? If this department cannot rise, China can hardly transfer to an innovative country. This process is not as fast as people thought. Considering the formation of human capital, the growth up of knowledge departments and the allocation by remuneration in the USA, China still needs a long time. Only through a series of education endeavors can we form an innovative department. After 30 or 40 years, China can only reach the knowledge innovation level of the USA in 1995. This also includes the serial system reform mentioned by the reports from Xiamen University.

We have compared the USA, South Korea, Mexico and China. From the perspective of consumption ratio, the USA has already reached certain level, and the South Korea is very close. The knowledge consumption of Mexico is low. In face, all kinds of ratios of the tertiary industry of Mexico are very high, but only the proportion of knowledge consumption is low, and therefore, the modern service like Science-Culture-Health-Physics in the whole tertiary industry is not high. So, how about the current China? China now is still more or less moving backward, and the reason is the monopoly regulation, which constrains the transformation process of the structure. As the consumption of Science, Culture, Health and Physics industry is very complicated, it's not only about the pricing problem of state-owned departments. It also involves the generalized service and personalized service. The proportion of education expenditures, private consumption in medical expenditures in Xiamen is only within 25 %, and 75 % is governmental consumption. What's the reason? Because what they want to solve is the generalized service and the supply of public goods, and this is also the important reason that we cannot simply conduct the market allocation. Now we want to build the innovative country. When we need the increase of human capital, we should gradually give the market more power and let more people gain more individual demands in the consumption.

Here, I'd like to restate the structural problem of middle-income period. Whether the heterogeneous sectors exists or not during one period, it couldn't be allocated by the market, and thus the structural problem appears. Even though the middle-income period basically enters into the modern departments, the prominent behavior of the structural problem is that the modern service departments have very strong properties of public goods. It is not only about the relationship between the market and government, but more important is about the relationship of government, market and society. Therefore, we cannot simply conduct the market allocation. China is more particular, as these departments are public utility departments and totally governmental departments, and they cannot satisfy the diversity demands in this period, especially the demand for increasing the human capital. Their intrinsic function is the reproduction of labor force, so we can improve the scale benefits by the way of "organization", however it is extremely unsuitable now and this is the biggest structural problem in current China.

Generally speaking, this issue is much more difficult than we have imaged, and the difficulties lie in the fact that the consumption related with the

Science-Culture-Health-PE has the justice problem, the property of public goods has the generalized service problem and individual demand problem. However, no matter how difficult it is, if we don't conduct the reform of current system, it's hardly to conduct the supply side reform, and China is hardly to go to achieve the innovation.

6.4 Professor Wang Luolin, Former Executive Vice President, Chinese Academy of Social Sciences

The report from Xiamen University is logical and coherent. It's not easy to make a clear forecast for this year. Here I'd like to give two suggestions.

Firstly, the policy suggestions are not specific enough. This report stresses that while reducing supply in some areas, the government should give particular emphasis to increase supply in other areas. But in this report, it's still not clear for those practical institutions to decide which areas to reduce supply and which to increase.

Secondly, according to the report, due to the economic slowdown, the processes of economy structure adjustment begins to slow down. For some extent, it is true, as some figures certainly show the slows down. But in my opinion, economic slowdown tends to promote structural adjustment. Originally, reform and structure adjustment should be implemented when the economic development is going well. But in fact, the government and enterprises are often forced to carry out structural adjustment when the economy encounters difficulties. For example, many enterprises would not like to improve innovation and technologies unless they face difficulties. There is certainly obvious progress in innovation and structure adjustment during the current economic hard times in China. Professor Gao Peiyong said that some fiscal difficulties would force the decentralization of the central to local. The government is motivated to make some adjustment and reform in the structure when facing economic difficulties. In this situation, we should not only rely on the existing figures. Thus, it's inappropriate to simply say that the economic slowdown should be prevented as it also slows down the structural adjustment.

As for my own opinion, I am impressed with three sentences after I learned the report and went through some documents and scholar's articles recently.

The first sentence is said by general secretary Xi Jinping at a meeting of the economic leading group. He stated that we should figure out what is the current situation, which means we should seek truth from facts. It seems that we should not only pay attention to seek truth from facts in the view of the current situation, but also the situation in the future and past few years, or at least since the new century. There has not been very clear understanding of policy from 2008 to 2010. At that time, the government work report said that double-digit growth in 2010 was a miracle. To a certain extent, is the serious excess capacity we face now the sequel of that "miracle"? There is not appropriate judgment and introspection at present. At least, we should be practical and realistic when doing research work. If not, it is hard to evaluate the current situation objectively.

The second sentence is from a British academic articles I read before, which said we should not waste the opportunity. The economic crisis and economic downturn is bad, of course. But especially for researchers or the department in charge of the economy, it happens to be a good opportunity to learn and improve. At this time, many contradictions overshadowed in the process of high-speed growth will begin to show up. It helps us to further study and explore every aspects of economy more clearly.

What is the reason for the unexpected economic downturn at present in China? There are all kinds of different arguments and some deep research is needed. In my opinion, the main reason is that the long-term pattern of growth is extensive and hasn't get timely adjustments and changes yet. The original pattern of growth is going to come to the end, but the new pattern of economic growth is far from forming. Transformation of economic growth mode is a natural process in the old market economy with the market competition and technology improvement. For the developing country like China, as the extensive growth mode is matched with highly security administration management system, the government must promote and change the management system. The former Soviet Union began discussing on changing the pattern of growth in the 1970s, but they still failed until the end of the Soviet Union. We advocated the transformation of growth mode and economic management system in the 1990s. It is entirely correct to implement the transformation of growth mode and economic management system together, but these two changes are incomplete until today. What are the reasons? I think that it's our management system has not been fundamentally changed. It doesn't mean that the government should only pay attention to reform, ignoring the economic growth. The most important thing is to make clear what underlying cause is at present.

The third sentence is also from an economist's article. He said that we could not deal with the problems in the twenty-first century with the view in the twentieth century. I totally agree with it. When we were in the twentieth century, we often studied the issues with the view of economists in the nineteenth century. In the twenty-first century, it's common to create a model and make formula in the academic field with the view of economists in the twentieth century. We should consider the new situation and problem happened in the whole world economy and domestic economy since the new century. Therefore, we should improve our research methods. To keep up with the changing situation, we should study the new rule of global economic development and the new phenomenon of China's economic growth. International scholars now have a lot of publications in this aspect, for example, a Japanese scholar says that all countries around the world have the "Japanese disease". So what is "Japanese disease"? Is it true that all countries have the "Japanese disease"? It is worth studying. Some scholars also said that China is in the downward cycles of Business Cycle Theory at present. We should also consider to what extent the Business Cycle Theory still applies to today's world and China economy.

6.5 Professor Huang, Zhiling, the Chief Economist, China Construction Bank

Many views in the report published by Xiamen University are consistent with our past judgment. I endorse those views, especially the argument on the friction of the supply and demand structure caused by the upgrade of demand structure and the rigidity of supply structure.

In recent years, China's economic structure has taken place significant and positive changes under the guidance of market mechanism and government, especially the traditional industry with low, or even negative growth. The growth of high-tech industry and strategic emerging industries is more than doubled compared with GDP growth, but in fact, it seems to bring about negative impacts rather than pleasant surprises. The reason may be various. There is a large scale of high energy consumption and pollution industry, mining industry, industries with excess capacity and low-end manufacturing. As these industries sustain at low speed or even atrophic growth in the structural adjustment, though satisfies market and policy expectations, they can still have a significant negative impact on GDP. Although on the whole, high technology industry, high-end equipment manufacturing industry, strategic emerging industries and services is getting better, its scale is far less than the distressed industries. As the positive contribution of the latter to GDP is not enough to completely offset the negative impact of the former, GDP growth continues to face a huge downward pressure. These may be the main reasons.

Firstly, according to the contribution of primary, secondary and tertiary industries to GDP, positive influence of industry to GDP has been weakening in recent years. The economic growth in China has been descending slowly since 2012 after a short sharp fluctuation caused by the global financial crisis in 2008. Since 2012, the economic operation has run within the range of 7–8 % in the most of the time, and the change of economic structure has become the main factors affecting economic operation. Industry drove 3.9 percentage of the GDP growth in the first quarter of 2012, and the contribution rate of industry to GDP was 44.8 %. Then, in the fourth quarter of 2015, the promotion of GDP growth fell to 2.1 percentage points, while the contribution rate fell to 30.4 %. The influence of agriculture in GDP basically remained stable. The promotion of GDP growth has maintained at 0.2 to 0.3 percentage points, and contribution rate has been around 4 % since 2012. Although the contribution rate of service industry to GDP has been rising, it's not enough to offset the effects of the industrial slowdown. From 2012 to 2015, the promotion of service sector to GDP growth grew by 0.4 percentage points, while the promotion of industry to GDP fell by 1.8 percentage points. The contribution of service sector to GDP grew by 12.5 percentage points, while the contribution of industry to GDP fell by 18.4 percentage points.

From the international experience, the importance of industry stability cannot be ignored. When Japan and Korea succeed to become the high-income countries, although the share of services increased steadily and the share of agriculture declined gradually, the share of industry maintained at around 40 %. Unlike Japan and South Korea, there is a common characteristic in GDP structure changes among some Latin American countries which failed to escape the middle-income trap. When per capita GDP reached 10,000 dollar, the proportion of industry fell too fast, forming the hollowing out of the secondary industry and sluggish economy development.

Secondly, though the industrial categories are complete in China, the structure of the industry is at a low level. In the process of structural adjustment of industrial upgrading, there exists a huge number of backward production capacity which is supposed to be eliminated. Meanwhile, for the advanced manufacturing industry and strategic emerging industries, which are supposed to develop rapidly, the technical threshold of the formation of scale industries is also high. The vitality of the industry depends on market demand, and the revenue growth rate can reflect the change of market demand. In terms of industry internal structure, China has the most complete industrial categories, which consist of three major categories, 41 main classes, and more than 700 subclasses. And manufacturing accounts for nearly 90 % of the whole industry income. Through the statistical analysis of all the subdivision of industry, we found that the industry whose current income growth exceeded 9 % accounted for only 14 % of the total industrial revenue, and the industry whose growth rate was between 6 and 8 % accounted for 21 % of industry revenue. Meanwhile, the industry whose growth rate was between 0 and 5 % of the industry accounted for 28 %. The industry with negative growth accounted for 36 % of industry revenue, especially black metal, petroleum, coal, electric power industries. In 2015, the growth rate of accumulated income of steel processing industry was -12.57 %, while the proportion of it in the whole industry reached 4.29 %. It means that the volume of the industrial sectors whose growth was significantly higher than GDP accounted for at most 14 % of the overall industry. Those industries whose growth rate was below 5 % were considered to increase with slow speed, accounting for 64 % of the overall industry. Rising industry increment is not enough to make up for the loss of slump and recession industry. It could make many people have the feeling of being in a poor economic situation. For example, the cumulative growth rate of the communication system and the equipment manufacturing industry was as high as 17.6 % in 2015, more than twice compared with GDP. However, it accounted for only 0.79 % of the overall industry, and the contribution rate of it to GDP was very limited.

Thirdly, from the particle degree of small class to observe the change of industrial structure adjustment, it can be found that the polarization phenomenon is obvious. However, it has a significantly different effect on employment. On the one hand, high pollution, high energy consumption and the traditional low-end manufacturing are in a state of atrophy. The revenue growth of 5 subsectors in black metal smelting and rolling processing industry declined sharply. The increase of steel rolling processing with the highest proportion was −12.57 %, which become the biggest drag. The rest of subsectors with massive negative growth include crude oil processing and coking, cement and flat glass, thermal power; copper rolling processing, mining, metallurgy, building professional equipment manufacturing, etc. All of these subsectors are in the front rank of the industries with the negative growth.

Because of the extensive and low-end characteristic, the labor-intensive industry is almost synonymous with these industries in straitened circumstances. It not only affects GDP growth but also puts strains on the employment and social stability. For example, the average annual number of workers in coal mining and steel industry was 4.42 and 3.62 million respectively, while the historical peak was 5.29 and 4.15 million in 2013. The high technology industry, on the other hand, has maintained strong growth momentum, especially the electronic and communication equipment manufacturing. The electronic and communication equipment manufacturing remained high-speed growth, such as the equipment for electronic products manufacturing, optical fiber and optical cable manufacturing, lithium ion battery and communications equipment manufacturing. The increase rate of those subdivision industries was over 12 %, significantly higher than the overall industrial level. It also represents the direction of industrial upgrading.

But the biggest characteristic of the advanced manufacturing industry and high-tech industry is the high threshold and technology substitution effect to labor. In the process of future economic adjustment, although the development of those industries could make up the market share which was lost by those backward and extensive industries, it can't reduce the amount of employment and structural stress. Although high technology industries absorb new jobs, it is still difficult to offset the downward pressure on employment in the traditional industry.

It is inevitable to undertake a certain amount of hardship in the process of economic structure transformation. How can we reduce the difficulties of structural adjustment, and achieve economic growth mode transformation? Economic structure upgrade is the core of economic restructuring, rather than statistical significance on the number of structural change. For traditional industry, the government should merger and reorganization and reform to achieve upgrade as far as possible. And for those zombie companies, the government only needs to improve the corresponding social security system and let the market clear. From the international experience, in the period of both economic crisis and active economic restructuring, asset restructuring and debt restructuring, including bankruptcy reorganization which undergoes judicial process is the basic form of handling enterprises problems. Meanwhile, the real sense of bankruptcy liquidation in aggrement with the law makes up a small proportion. This operation can not only reduce the difficulties, but also increase the stock of resource utilization.

In the process of the economic structure adjustment, the existing stock of labor structure is difficult to meet the needs for labor in the new economy. The pressure of job transfer is significant and challenging. Thus, the government must take the responsibility to carry out the job-transfer training and re-employment guidance. Some international experience is worth to use for reference. For example, Japan formulated a series of action when it eliminated outdated industrial capacity. It mainly provided employment information service, employment guidance and vocational training and subsidies. Meanwhile, the government provided the original enterprise of workers with subsidies and training fees to extend the time of payment of unemployed insurance. It also arranged the unemployed persons to participate in public utilities, etc. When the United States dealt with the unemployment problem in the process of removing the excess capacity, it gradually established a modern welfare system and re-employment training system. The unemployment insurance system, on the one hand, guaranteed the basic life of the unemployed, on the other hand, it enhanced the function of unemployment prevention and re-employment promotion. South Korea has established the employment insurance system before the Asian financial crisis, mainly including the unemployment insurance system, the stable employment and professional skills development plans. Germany began "50 + " plan from 2006, to solve the employment problem of older workers over the age of 50, and support the transformation from first and second industry to service industry. The main content of the plan included "composite wage" project. It means that the government provided wage subsidies for those unemployed older workers who were willing to accept jobs with less salary before unemployment and it also relieved 90 % of endowment insurance payment in 2 years of such workers. Meanwhile, the government also provided those enterprises which hired older workers with 1–3 years of subsidy that was about 30–50 % of wages. And it also provided older workers who quit their post to take care of an old man with about 30 % of salary, and 50 % of salary to those who took care of the non-related elderly. This plan significantly increased the employment of older population to 55 %. These experiences are worthy of our serious study. The Central has decided to set up special funds, mainly for the laid-off personnel placement in the steel and coal industry, which is targeted measures. At the same time, we also look forward to all levels of government can indeed take the responsibility of re-employment guidance and skills training in the process of economic structure transformation.

6.6 Professor Hwa, Erh-Cheng, the Chief Economist, Baoshang Bank

I'd like to talk about the management of the supply side. From the general law of economic development, developing economies should pay attention to the supply side while developed economies mainly focus on the reform of demand side. As the potential economic growth in developing countries is quite high, economic management certainly should pay attention to bringing all potentialities into full play. The development potential of developed countries has been relatively small. Therefore, the economy management in developed countries mostly pay attention to demand management and how to promote economic stability, rather than the economic development potential. In the international economic organization, the work of international monetary fund is mainly aggregate demand management in order to maintain the macroeconomic stability in the short term. When the country falls into crisis, it provides assistance with the monetary and fiscal policy to restore economic stability. The World Bank, which is an economic development agency, mainly serves developing countries and tries to improve economic development potential in these countries. International economic organizations also have such a division of labor. IMF focuses on the demand side, while the World Bank focuses on the supply side.

Generally speaking, developed countries focus on the demand side, while developing countries should pay attention to the supply side. However, the economic performance mostly is affected by both supply and demand factors. Therefore, if we don't pay attention to them in advance, it is hard to find that the decline in growth is caused by whether the supply side or demand side.

If supply side caused the problem, it's useless to stimulate economic growth with aggregate demand management and future trouble will be boundless, such as the soaring debts. Since 2008 economic recovery in the developed economies with unprecedented monetary stimulation has been very limited so far. Do these countries fall in stagnation? In this case, the government should introduce some supply-side policies which mean structural adjustment policies, rather than rely on monetary policy.

We should figure out whether the problem of China's economy is caused by the demand side or supply side. The economic growth was high in the century before the global financial crisis, but the structure was unbalanced. In 2007, the proportion of the trade surplus in GDP reached a peak of almost 8 %, and the economic growth rate reached a peak of 14 %. After the outbreak of the global financial crisis, the rapid growth of the economic structure imbalance turned out to be unsustainable. After that, China's economic experienced the structural adjustment, which shifted from an imbalance and unsustainable condition to a rebalancing and sustainable state. The rebalancing of a total demand structure shifted the main pulling power of demand growth from foreign trade to domestic demand. From the side of domestic demand, the proportion of household income in GDP began to rebound since 2011, which strongly promoted the transformation of the main pulling power of domestic demand from investment to consumption. This trend continues now. The cost of economic structure re-balance is the economic growth slowdown.

At the same time, the supply side has also experienced structural adjustment. China's economic growth slowdown mainly caused by the decline in growth rate of labor productivity. As the average annual growth rate of employment exceeded 3.0 % in the 1980s and plunged to 0.4 % in this century, it has not been the main factors of economic growth. Why did the labor productivity growth rate decrease? Over the past few years, the labor productivity of industry and services has been falling, especially industry. The national labor productivity growth rate has fallen dramatically from 10 to 7 % from 2010 to 2014. The contribution of industry to the national labor productivity growth fell to 4.6 % from 7.3 %, which almost entirely explained the decline in the national labor productivity growth. Meanwhile, the contribution rate of service industry only decreased from 2.5 to 2.3 %.

The other reason is that agricultural employment has accelerated to move to service after the financial crisis. The proportion of agricultural employment in the national employment has fallen by 9 %. Among it, 6 % of the rural population flows to services, while 3 % to the industry. As industry labor productivity is higher than the service, when more and more surplus rural population flow to the service sector, rather than the industries, it's inevitable to lead to the decline in the national labor productivity.

I think the status of the labor market is a crucial observation points to figure out whether the problem of the China economy is caused by supply side or demand side. In a completely competitive market, the real wage growth of a worker should match his labor productivity growth. However, since 2011, the actual growth of the national income has exceeded the labor productivity, and unit labor costs have been rising. It turns out that the labor market is the seller's market, rather than the buyer's market. At the same time, the steady growth of employment in cities is consistent with labor force growth. The stability of the labor market fully illustrates that the downward pressure of economic growth does not come from the insufficient aggregate demand. And the extra demand side policy stimulation is unnecessary.

The rising of unit labor costs leads to the increasing proportion of national income in GDP. Meanwhile, it reverses the long decline trend and supports the transformation of the main pulling power of demand-side from investment to consumption. Therefore, the structure of the demand side and supply side change has been highly consistent since 2011. At the same time, corporate profits are squeezed, forcing enterprises to improve the labor productivity. Thus, the Chinese economy began to experience the transformation and upgrade of economic structure.

As the decline in the economic growth is the problem of supply side, the supply side reform is crucial. The reform of the supply side aims to create effective supply and lead the new requirements. As Apple computer's late CEO Steve Jobs said, the product should focus on innovation and drive the demand of the market.

China's economy has entered the process of industrialization, centering on the urbanization. Meanwhile, the industrial growth continues to rise, and it becomes a middle-income country. Labor productivity of industrial enterprises will continue to improve in the future, and also release surplus labor force to services. More and more labor force will flow to the service sector, which is the post-industrial period dominated by services. The main premise of the structure adjustment is to break through the middle-income trap. According to the analysis of the World Bank, over the past 50 or 60 years, there have been only a few countries going across the middle-income trap.

Therefore, implementing the reform of the supply side is supposed to promote labor productivity and support the transformation and upgrade of economic structure adjustment with the improvement of investment efficiency. The proportion of investment in GDP reached 50 % after the financial crisis. Such high investment rate did not bring economic growth. Instead, the economic growth continued to slow down. The main reason is that the marginal productivity of investment continued to decline. It also means a fall in investment and financing efficiency, because investment needs funding, whether directly or indirectly. Then, it could lead to the rising debt and continuous economic slowdown. Therefore, while the government encourages the real economy innovations and the stock revitalization, improving the efficiency of investment and financing is also the important content of the reform of the supply side. The government is supposed vigorously to promote the reform of financial system and the development of financial markets, expand direct financing channels and improve the ability of financial market risk pricing.

Chapter 7
The Macroeconomic Situation and Policy of China in 2016: A Report on the Questionnaire Survey (2016.2.No.6)

To keep abreast of the macroeconomic situation and policy trend, an annual questionnaire survey of China's macroeconomic situation and policy jointly started twice a year since the first time in August 2013, held by *the Economic Information Daily*, Xinhua News Agency and the Center for Macroeconomic Research, Xiamen University (one of the Key Research Institutes of Humanities and Social Sciences of the Ministry of Education of China). This is the sixth time questionnaire survey about the study. There were 20 questions directly about China's macroeconomic situation and policy trend in the questionnaire, and we invited some domestic economists in relevant area for this survey by email in the late of January 2016, and finally got responses from 121 of them. This survey offered the latest understandings and judgments of experts concerning the economic situation of the world, trends of some major indicators about China's macro-economy, trends of China's macroeconomic policies in 2016 and structural reforms in the supply side of China. The results of this survey are presented as follows:

7.1 The Economic Situation of the World in 2016

In accordance with the latest economic forecast of the IMF on January 19, the economic growth rate of USA would be 2.6 % in 2016, while it was about 2.5 % in 2015. Hence, we conducted a questionnaire survey on the trend of USA's economic growth. The survey reflected that 57 % of the experts answered that the economic growth rate of USA would be "between 2.1 % and 2.5 %" in 2016. Thirty nine percent claimed that it would be "between 2.6 and 3.0 %". Two percent expected that it would be "below 2.1 %". Two percent of the experts thought that it would be "between 3.1 % and 3.5 %" and no one considered the rate would be "3.5 % or more". In sum, nearly 60 % of the experts thought that the economic growth rate of USA would show a slow downward trend in 2016, while more than 40 % of the

© Springer Science+Business Media Singapore 2016

Center for Macroeconomic Research of Xiamen University, *China's Macroeconomic Outlook*, Current Chinese Economic Report Series, DOI 10.1007/978-981-10-2068-1_7

experts believed it would be in recovery in 2016, whose expectation was more optimistic than IMF's.

In accordance with the latest economic forecast of the IMF on January 19, the economic growth rate of Euro zone would be 1.7 % in 2016, while it was 1.5 % in 2015. We also conducted a questionnaire survey on the trend of Euro zone's economic growth. The survey reflected that 75 % of the experts estimated the number would be "between 1.3 % and 1.6 %" in 2016. Nineteen percent claimed that it would be "between 1.7 % and 2.0 %". Six percent of the experts thought that it would be "below 1.3 %"and no experts chose "between 2.1 % and 2.4 %" or "2.4 % or more". In sum, more than 80 % of the experts expressing a relatively optimistic expectation believed that the economy of Euro zone would show a slow downward trend in 2016. But nearly 20 % of the experts believed it would be in recovery in 2016.

In addition, we conducted a questionnaire survey on the number of times and when USA would choose to raise interest rates in 2016. In 115 valid questionnaires, the survey reflected that 55 % of the experts estimated the number would be once in 2016. Thirty-five percent claimed it would be twice in 2016. Three percent considered third times and 2 % chose four times. Moreover, 55 % of the experts thought that the USA would do so in the first half of 2016. While 40 % of the experts believed it would take place in the second half of 2016.

7.2 The Forecast of Some Major Indicators of China's Macro-Economy in 2016

According to the preliminary accounting data provided by the Bureau of Statistics on January 19, in 2015, China's GDP increased 6.9 % as high as that in 2014. How about the growth rate of China's GDP in 2016? The survey showed that 76 % of the experts thought that it would be "between 6.5 % and 6.8 %", 12 % expected that it would be "between 6.8 % and 7.0 %", 8 % chose "6.5 % or less" and 3 % of the experts chose "7 % or more". In sum, more than 80 % of the experts considered China's economic growth would continue to slide in 2016.

In 2015, China's CPI increased 1.4 % as high as that in 2014. How about the trend of China's CPI in 2016? The survey showed that 63 % of the experts expected it to be "between 1.4 % and 1.8 %", 22 % thought that it might be "between 0.9 % and 1.3 %", 13 % held the view that it would be "between 1.9 % and 2.3 %", 2 % chose "0.9 % or less". In sum, considering the fact that the CPI increased by 1.4 % in 2015, more than three quarters of the experts forecasted a certain upward trend in 2016. But quarter of the experts believed that the price level would continue to decline and the deflationary pressure would rise further in 2016.

In 2015, China's PPI decreased 5.2 % as high as that in 2014. How about the trend of China's PPI in 2016? The survey showed that 40 % of the experts expected it to be "between −5.2 % and −4.2 %",26 % thought that it might be "between

−6.2 % and −5.3 %", 21 % held the view that it would be "between −4.1 % and −3.2 %", 4 % chose "−6.2 % or less", and 9 % claimed that it would be "-3.2 % or more". Considering the fact China's PPI in 2015 decreased 5.2 % as high as that in 2014, 70 % of the experts estimated that the falls in China's PPI would gradually slow in 2016. But 30 % of the experts claimed that the falls would continue to expand in 2016.

On August 11, 2015, The People's Bank of China launched the reform of pricing mechanism of RMB exchange rate, up to December 31,2015, the USD to CNY (RMB) exchange rate was about 6.4936, the CNY(RMB) to USD exchange rate was down nearly 6 % throughout the year 2015. Considering the relatively strong devaluation expectation of RMB, how about the trend and range of the CNY (RMB) to USD exchange rate in 2016? The survey showed that 45 % of the experts expected it would "continue to depreciate by 3 % to 6.6884", 35 % considered it would "continue to depreciate by 6 % to 6.8832", 10 % of the experts thought it would "keep steady", 4 % claimed it would meet "slight revaluation by 2 % to 6.3637". In addition, 6 % of the experts put forward different views, such as "depreciating to 7.0", "continuing to depreciate by 4 % to 6.73", "continuing to depreciate by 10 % to 7.1", "depreciating at the beginning and then keeping steady between 6.85 and 6.40". In sum, more than 80 % of the experts forecasted a continuous trend of depreciation of the RMB against the USD in 2016.

In accordance with the household survey on the unity of city and countryside, China's residents' per capita disposable income rose by 8.9 % year-on-year in2015 (the real growth was 7.4 % after deducting the price factor), in which the per capita disposable income of urban residents rose by 8.2 % year-on-year (the real growth was 6.6 %); the per capita disposable income of rural residents rose by 8.9 % year-on-year (the real growth was 7.5 %). How about the trend of the year-on-year nominal growth of China's residents' per capita disposable income in 2016? The survey showed that 53 % of the experts thought "the growth of the per capita disposable income of urban residents will be lower than 2015's 8.2 % and the growth of the per capita disposable income of rural residents will be lower than 2015's 8.9 %", 21 % considered that "the growth of the per capita disposable income of urban residents will be higher than 2015's 8.2 % and the growth of the per capita disposable income of rural residents will be higher than 2015's 8.9 %", 19 % held the view that "the growth of the per capita disposable income of urban residents will be lower than 2015's 8.2 % and the growth of the per capita disposable income of rural residents will be higher than 2015's 8.9 %", 7 % chose "the growth of the per capita disposable income of urban residents will be higher than 2015's 8.2 % and the growth of the per capita disposable income of rural residents will be lower than 2015's 8.9 %". In sum, more than half of the experts considered that China's residents' per capita disposable income would decline in 2016. But 20 % of the experts thought that China's residents' per capita disposable income would increase in 2016.

China's fixed investment (deducting farmers) in 2015 was about 55.16 trillion yuan, with a year-on-year growth of 10 % (the real growth was 12 % after deducting the price factor). How about the growth of China's fixed investments in 2016?

the survey showed that 32 % of the experts expected the total fixed investments would increase year-on-year at the rate "between 9.0 % and 9.9 %", 26 % considered that it would increase at the rate "between 10.0 % and 11.0 %", 16 % chose "between 11.1 and 12.0 %", 17 % thought that the growth rate would be "12.0 % or more", and 9 % claimed that it would be "less than 9.0 %". In sum, nearly 60 % of experts maintained that the growth of China's fixed investments would continue to rise in 2016 considering the fact that the year-on-year nominal growth of China's fixed investments was 10 % in 2015. But more than 40 % of the experts believed that the growth of China's fixed investments would slide in 2016.

Comparing with the slowdown of the economy and investment growth, the investment in real estate market in 2015 was 9.60 trillion yuan with a year-on-year growth of 1.0 % (the real growth was 2.8 % after deducting the price factor). How about the growth rate of China's investment in real estate market in 2016? The survey showed that 66 % of the experts expected it would be "between 0.1 % and 3.0 %", 18 % expected that it would be "between -5 % and 0 %", 12 % claimed that it would be "between 3.1 % and 5.0 %", 2 % maintained that it would be "between 5.1 % and 8.0 %" and 2 % expected that it would be "more than 8 %". In sum, more than 80 % of the experts forecasted a upward trend of the investment in real estate market in 2016 considering the fact that the growth rate of China's investment in real estate market was 1.0 % in 2015. But nearly 20 % of the experts thought that the investment in real estate market would post negative growth in 2016.

China's total retail sales of consumer goods in 2015 were 30.09 trillion yuan with a year-on-year growth of 10.7 %. How about the growth rate of China's total retail sales of consumer goods in 2016? The survey showed that 64 % of the experts expected the total retail sales of consumer goods would increase year on year at the rate "between 10.1 % and 11 %", 18 % considered that it would increase at the rate "between 11.1 % and 12 %", 15 % chose "10 % or less", 2 % of experts held the view that it would be "between 12.1 % and 13 %" and only 1 % claimed that it would be "more than 13 %". The results reflected that more than 80 % of the experts maintained that the growth of the total retail sales of consumer goods would increase in 2016 considering the fact that the nominal growth was 10.7 % in 2015. But 15 % of the experts thought it would decline in 2016.

China's total exports in dollar terms decreased obviously by 2.5 % in 2015 than in 2014. How about the growth rate of China's total exports in 2016? The survey showed that 35 % of the experts expected the total exports in dollar terms would increase "between −2.5 % and −0.1 %", 35 % considered that it would increase "between 0 % and 2.5 %", 26 % chose "between −5.0 % and −2.6 %", 2 % held the view that it would be "less than −5.0 %", 2 % thought it would be "more than 2.5 %". In sum, the results reflected that 70 % of the experts believed that the growth of the total exports would maintain a certain degree of rise in 2016 considering the fact that the total exports in dollar terms fell by 2.5 % in 2015 than in 2014. But more than quarter of the experts thought that the growth of the total exports would continue to decline in 2016.

China's total imports in dollar terms fell by 14.0 % in 2015 than in 2014, and it also decreased significantly. How about the growth rate of China's total imports in

2016? The survey showed that 36 % of the experts expected the total imports in dollar terms would increase "between −14.0 % and −9.0 %", 26 % considered that it would increase between −9.0 % and −4.0 %", 16 % chose "between −15.1 % and −14.1 %", 12 % held the view that it would be "more than −4.0 %", 10 % thought it would be "less than −15.1 %". In sum, the results reflected that three quarters of the experts believed that the growth of China's imports would rise in 2016 considering the fact that the total imports in dollar terms fell by 14.0 % in 2015 than in 2014. But more than quarter of the experts believed that the growth of China's imports would continue to decline in 2016.

7.3 The Macroeconomic Policies May Be Taken by China in the Future

China's broad monetary supply (M2) in 2015 was 139.23 trillion yuan, with a year-on-year growth of 13.3 %. How about the growth rate of China's M2 in 2016? The survey showed that 43 % of the experts had the expectation that it grow "between 13.3 % and 14.3 %". Twenty-nine percent considered "between 12.2 % and 13.2 %". Fourteen percent chose "between 11.1 % and 12.1 %", 14 % of experts maintained "14.4 % or more" and 2 % of the experts thought that it would be "11.1 % or less". Considering that China's broad monetary supply (M2) in 2015 had a year-on-year growth of 13.3 %, the results reflected that nearly 60 % of experts thought that the growth rate of M2 would rise in 2016. It probably means the central bank of China would continue to keep a moderate loose monetary policy in 2016.

Will the central bank of China continue to lower the deposit-reserve ratio in 2016? If yes, when will it happen?In 117 valid questionnaires, 45 % of experts expected that the central bank would lower the deposit-reserve ratio in the first quarter of 2016, 31 % maintained that it would be in the second quarter, 12 % thought that it would happen in the second half of 2016 and 8 % believed that it would not happen in 2016. Overall, nearly 90 % of experts considered that the central bank would continue to lower the deposit-reserve ratio in 2016 which possibly signaled that the central bank of China would keep a moderately loose monetary policy in 2016.

Will the central bank of China cut the benchmark interest rate in 2016? If yes, when will it happen?In 108 valid questionnaires, 31 % of experts thought that the central bank of China would cut the benchmark interest rate in the second quarter, 23 % chose "the first quarter", 21 % maintained it would be in the second half of 2016 and 13 % thought that it would not happen in 2016. The results reflected that more than three quarters of experts considered that the central bank would continue to cut the benchmark interest rate in 2016 which provided further evidence that the central bank of China would keep a moderately loose monetary policy in 2016.

China's new loans were 11.72 trillion yuan in 2015, with a year-on-year growth of 1.81 trillion yuan. How about the change trend of the scale of new loans in 2016? The survey reflected that 70 % of experts expected it would be "more than 11.72 trillion yuan", 18 % held the view that it would be "less than 11.72 trillion yuan", 12 % chose "not determinable". Generally, 70 % of experts claimed that the scale of new loans would continue to increase in 2016 which further indicated that the central bank of China would keep a moderately loose monetary policy in 2016.

The working conference of the People's Bank of China in January 8 proposed that China would continue to implement prudent monetary policy in 2016. What are the specific measures? The survey showed that 83 % of the experts maintained that it would continue to deepen the reform of interest rate marketing, further to improve exchange rate mechanism, and keep exchange rate of RMB basically stable at a reasonable and balanced level, 67 % of the experts thought that it would continue to use the monetary policy instruments to lower the funding cost, such as pledged supplementary lending (PSL),medium-term lending facilities (MLF), credit asset pledged relending policy and so on, 65 % of the experts held the view that it would standardize the development of small loan companies, private lending, and Internet finance with policy and low constraints, open up inter-bank market seriously; 62 % of the experts considered that it would build up the market interest rate formation and regulation mechanism, and improve the effectiveness of central bank regulation on market rate; 59 % claimed that it would develop Macro Prudential policy framework, and explore the establishment of Macro Prudential Assessment (MPA) system; 48 % of the experts supported providing accurate financial services for poverty alleviation according to structural tax reductions and cut fees across the board; 36 % of the experts believed being deeply involved in global economic and financial governance, continuing to promote two-way opening of the financial sector. In addition, 3 % of the experts put forward other views, including: reducing the rate of interest paid on excess reserves until undertaking negative deposit interest rate; restricting the development of private banking and underground financial business; improving regulation of the stock and securities market, especially consummating the mechanism of entering and withdrawing for financial markets.

In terms of fiscal policy, a questionnaire survey based on the possible space of fiscal policy in 2016 was conducted. The survey showed that 85 % of experts expected it would further implement the policy of tax reduction, in order to give enterprises and market players more available funds; 66 % held the view that it would increase the deficit rate periodically, expand the size of budget deficit moderately and increase the scale of treasury bond correspondingly, 63 % chose that it would optimize the structure of fiscal expenditure, cut down general expenditure of public funds and spend more on people's livelihood according to the principle of sustainability and insurance, 61 % considered that it would accelerate the comprehensive use of financial capital, vitalize the inventory of fiscal funds, and improve the efficiency of fund utilizing, 55 % of experts thought that it would issue local government bonds to replace existing obligation and handle the relationship between debt risk and steady growth, 52 % maintained it would actively extend the cooperation mode between government and social capital (PPP) which would be utilized to support transportation, public utilities and other infrastructure investments, 45 % thought that it would accelerate to replace the business tax with a value-added tax in construction industry, real estate industry and financial industry, and reduce the effective tax rate of enterprise, 39 % of experts claimed that it would expand the scale of long-term construction bond, and guide the investment orientation of bank loans and private investment through discount loans, capital allowance and other measures. Furthermore, 2 % of experts put forward other views, including: supporting the development of state owned enterprises; reducing the profit space of private production; setting up special fiscal expenditure of ecological civilization and valley harnessing.

7.4 Supply-Side Structural Reforms

The Central Economic Work Conference in 2015 stressed the need to promote supply-side structural reforms which consists of the macro and micro levels. Our project team conducted a questionnaire survey about the important areas of supply-side structural reforms. The survey indicated that 72 % of the experts expected it should improve product quality to improve the supply structure of products, expand the effective supply, strictly control the new capacity, eliminate backward production capacity and transform capacity with good benefits to dissolve excess capacity; 69 % thought that it might promote institutional innovation, and actively promote innovation, entrepreneurship and Internet+, upgrade industry to promote the new consumption and supply and create new economic growth point; 67 % held the view that the key was to improve the current imbalance of supply and demand for product structure and the phenomenon of excessive capacity and insufficient effective supply; 64 % chose that accelerating the reforms of monopoly field and allowing private capital participate in the competition in monopoly industries in the form of sole proprietorship or mixed ownership are important; 62 % claimed that it should further accelerate the reform of the factors of the market, optimize the allocation of resources, and promote the improvement of factor productivity; 61 % of experts considered that setting up the mechanism of evolution with the market as the guidance to retain the beneficial enterprise and eliminate "zombie" companies with low efficiency in market competition was an effective approach; 60 % held the view that government should streamline administration and delegate more power to lower levels and give full play to the fundamental role of the market in resource allocation; 52 % of experts believed that it should speed up the reform of structural tax; 40 % of experts thought that what should be done now is to accelerate the urbanization of rural migrant workers for the purpose of enlarging effective demand and digesting inventory. Furthermore, other policies were put forward by 3 % of experts: fully implementing development strategy driven by innovation; deepening the reform of scientific research; promoting the conversion of scientific research achievements and innovation ability; canceling the one-child policy to increase labor supply; improving and optimizing the functions of the government to foster effective demand rather than eliminating backward production capacity in a recession; establishing lots of new state-owned enterprises, etc.

From the micro-level in terms of the supply-side structural reforms, what is needed is to further open factor market, optimize resource allocation and improve total factor productivity, which was also investigated in this survey. Eight three percent of experts maintained that it should further broaden access, which means that new investors should be introduced to compete in monopoly industries such as oil, gas, power, telecommunications, railways; 81 % of the experts believed that in order to promote the flow of innovative factors and cultivate human capital, it should focus on creating an institutional environment conducive to innovation and protecting intellectual property rights, especially intellectual property rights; 72 % of the experts held the view that the focus is to accelerate the flow of land, capital, personnel and other factors of urban and rural areas and optimize allocation; 71 % of experts considered that we should rise to the high-end global value chains by pushing the manufacturing industry from extensive management to exquisite production; 65 % of the experts considered that excess capacity should be squeezed out through the survival of the fittest, and all regions were needed to reduce the corresponding capacity in accordance with the existing production capacity with the permission of quota trading. At the same time, actively promoting mergers and acquisitions led by the dominant enterprises was necessary. Furthermore, other views were put forward by 3 % of experts: deepening the reform of state-owned enterprises and developing private economy while combining reforms of property rights system with reconstruction of resource allocation mechanism and digestion of excess capacity; reforming the government wage system and improving the incentive mechanism of government officials; breaking the barriers between regions to establish a compensation mechanism, in which factors can fully flow and be used; vigorously promoting the policy about integration of urban and rural education to improve labor stock; expanding the scope of the private economy, especially in areas such as financial, cultural, livelihood and service.

According to the Chinese Pinyin order of their names, the 121 experts who joined this questionnaire survey were: Bai Peiwen, Chang Xin, Chen Changbing, Chen Gong, Chen Jianbao, Chen Kunting, Chen Langnan, Chen Menggen, Chen Shoudong, Chen Xue Bin, Chen Yanbin, Chen Zhao, Chen Zhiyong, Dai Kuizao, Fan Conglai, Fan Ziying, Gao Bo, Gao Peiyong, Geng Qiang, Guo Qiyou, Guo Xibao, Guo Xiaohe, Guo Zhiyi, Han Zhaozhou, He Jingtong, Hu Xiaoping, Huang Jianzhong, Huang Maoxing, Jian Xinhua, Jiang Yongmu, Li Chong, Li Jianwei, Li Jun, Li Laya, Li Shantong, Li Shi, Li Xiao, Li Xuesong, Li Yingdong, Lin Shu, Lin Xuegui, Liu Dong, Liu Fengliang, Liu Jianping, Liu Jinquan, Liu Qiongzhi,

Liu Shujie, Liu Xiliang, Liu Xiahui, Liu Xiaoxin, Liu Yunzhong, Liu Zhibiao, Lu Ming, Ma Ying, Feng Jinju, Peng Shuijun, Peng Suling, Qiu Chongming, Qu Wanwen Ren Baoping, Shen Kunrong, Shi Gang, Song Li, Su Jian, Sun Wei, Tang Jijun, Wang Changyun, Wang Tongsan, Wang Yida, Wang Cheng, Wang Dashu, Wang Haijie, Wang Jiping, Wang Jinzhao, Wang Liyong, Wang Meijin, Wang Xi, Wang Yiming, Wang Yuesheng, Wen Chuanhao, Wu Xinru, Xiao Xingzhi, Xie Pan, Xu Jianguo, Xu Yifan, Xu Wenbin, Xu Xianchun, Yang Can, Yang Chengyu, Yang Ruilong, Yang Zhiyong, Yi Xianrong, Yin Xingmin, Yu Li, Yu Zuo, Yuan Fuhua, Zang Xuheng, Zeng Jinli, Zeng Kanghua, Zeng Wuyi, Zhang Chengsi, Zhang Donghui, Zhang Liqun, Zhang Liancheng, Zhang Long, Zhang Mingzhi, Zhang Monan, Zhang Ping, Zhao Xiaolei, Zhao Xindong, Zhao Zhenquan, Zhao Zhijun, Zheng Chaoyu, Zheng Tingguo, Zhong Chunping, Zhou Liqun, Zhou Zejiong, Zhu Baohua, Zhu Jianping, Zhu Qigui, Zhuang Zongming.

The experts who joined this questionnaire survey are from institutions like Ministry of Finance, National Development and Reform Commission, China's National Bureau of Statistics, Macroeconomic Research Department of Development Research Center of the State Council, Social Development Research Department of Development Research Center of the State Council, Development Strategy and Regional Economic Research Department of Development Research Center of the State Council, The Ministry of Commerce, the China Center for international economic exchanges, National Academy of Economic Strategy of CASS, The Institute of Finance and Banking of CASS, The Institute of Economics of CASS, The Institute of World Economy and Politics of CASS, The Institute of Quantitative Economics and Technical Economics of Chinese Academy of Social Sciences, Taiwan Academia Sinica, Taiwan Chung-Hua Institution for Economic Research and universities like Anhui Finance and Economics University, Peking University, Beijing Normal University, ChongqingTechnology and Business University, Dongbei University of Finance and Economics, Fudan University, Fujian Normal University, East China Normal University, Huaqiao University, Huazhong University of Science and Technology, Jilin University, Jinan University, Lanzhou University, Nanjing University of Finances and Economics, Nanjing University, Nankai University, Tsinghua University, Shandong University, Shaanxi Normal University, Shanghai University of Finance and Economics, Shanghai University of International Business and Economics, Shanghai Jiao Tong University, Capital University of Economics and Business, Sichuan University, National Taiwan University, Tianjin University of Finance and Economics, Tianjin University of Commerce, Wuhan University, Xi'an Jiao Tong University, Northwest University, Southwestern University of Finance and Economics, Xiamen University, National University of Singapore, Zhejiang University of Finance and Economics, Zhejiang University of Technology, Zhengzhou University, Renmin University of China, Zhongnan University of Economics and Law, Sun Yat-Sen University, Central University of Finance and Economics, etc.

Finally, we thank for the active participation and insights of these experts mentioned above sincerely.

Statistics comparison of the forecast by research group with the forecast by 121 experts on major indicators of China's macro-economy

Major indicators of China's macro-economy in 2016	Forecast by research Group (%)	The interval and ratio of forecast by experts (%)	
		Interval	Ratio
The growth rate of China's GDP	6.66	6.5 to 6.8	76
The growth rate of China's CPI	1.48	1.4 to 1.8	63
The growth rate of China's PPI	−3.31	−6.2 to −5.3	26
		−5.2 to −4.2	40
		−4.2 to −3.2	21
Nominal growth of China's total retail sales of consumer goods	11.53	10.1 to 11.0	64
		11.1 to 12.0	18
Nominal growth of China's fixed investments	9.13	9.0 to 9.9	32
		10.0 to 1.0	26
Nominal growth of China's export in dollar terms	0.83	0.0 to 2.5	35
		−2.5 to −0.1	35
		−5.0 to −2.6	26

Appendix: Model Specification and Analysis

Based on the purpose of the analysis, assuming there are two kinds of consumer good in the economy C_{1t} and C_{2t}, Y_{1t} and Y_{2t} are two types of manufacturer. Among them, C_{1t} represents physical products; its production is in a state of perfect competition. C_{2t} represents service offerings, which is constrained by institution; its production is in a state of complete monopoly. The greatest difference between perfect competition and monopoly is that the former involves a price taker, whereby the producer does not have the ability to adjust prices and therefore realizes profit maximization mainly through production adjustment; in the latter, the producer can not only choose to adjust prices but can also realize profit maximization via production adjustment. To restrict the monopolist's price adjustment capacity, we assume that monopolists have price adjustment costs.

1. Representative households

There are countless families with indefinite lives in the economy. Every family has one unit of time endowment. Representative households maximize their lifetime expected utility:

$$E_0\Big[\sum_{t=0}^{\infty}\beta^t U(C_t,N_t)\Big], 0<\beta<1. \tag{1}$$

where E is the control variable of conditional expectation, β is the discount factor, N_t is the working time, C_t represents a total weighted consumption index that represents two types of consumer good. The weighted formula is

$$C_t=\left[\theta^{1/\varepsilon}C_{1t}^{\frac{\varepsilon-1}{\varepsilon}}+(1-\theta)^{1/\varepsilon}C_{2t}^{\frac{\varepsilon-1}{\varepsilon}}\right]^{\frac{\varepsilon}{\varepsilon-1}}. \tag{2}$$

where C_{1t} is the consumption of physical products, C_{2t} is the consumption of services, θ is the share of physical products out of the total consumption index

© Springer Science+Business Media Singapore 2016

Center for Macroeconomic Research of Xiamen University, *China's Macroeconomic Outlook*, Current Chinese Economic Report Series, DOI 10.1007/978-981-10-2068-1 reflecting the tendency of the consumption structure, ε is the elasticity of the substitution of the two types of product consumption. If $\varepsilon > 1$, they are substitutes.

Restricted by the total expenditure, maximizing the total consumption, representative households' first-order conditions for C_{1t} and C_{2t} are

$$C_{1t} = \theta\left(\frac{P_{1t}}{P_t}\right)^{-\varepsilon} C_t. \tag{3}$$

$$C_{2t} = (1-\theta)\left(\frac{P_{2t}}{P_t}\right)^{-\varepsilon} C_t. \tag{4}$$

where P_{1t} is the price of physical products, P_{2t} is the price of services, and P_t is the total weighted price index. Based on the above setting, we can easily obtain

$$P_t = \left[\theta P_{1t}^{1-\varepsilon} + (1-\theta)P_{2t}^{1-\varepsilon}\right]^{\frac{1}{1-\varepsilon}}. \tag{5}$$

Dividing Eq. (3) by Eq. (4), we obtain when total consumption is maximized, the best ratio of the consumption of the two types of products is

$$\frac{C_{1t}}{C_{2t}} = \frac{\theta}{1-\theta}\left(\frac{P_{1t}}{P_{2t}}\right)^{-\varepsilon}. \tag{6}$$

We know that the optimal consumption ratio depends on the consumption weights of the two types of product, relative prices, and the elasticity of substitution.

Further, we assume the form of utility function is CRRA for the representative households:

$$U = \frac{C_t^{1-\sigma}}{1-\sigma} - \frac{N_t^{1+\gamma}}{1+\gamma}. \tag{7}$$

where σ represents the coefficient of consumers' relative risk aversion, equal to the reciprocal of the consumption intertemporal substitution elasticity, γ represents the reciprocal of labor elasticity of intertemporal substitution.

To simplify the analysis, we assume that the representative households do not invest but hold bonds. In period t, the number of due bonds the households hold are B_t, which means B_t units of income; meanwhile, using nominal cost $1/R_t$ to purchase B_{t+1} units of new bonds, $R_t = 1 + r_t$, r_t is the nominal interest rate from period t to period $t+1$; in period, the family supplies N_{it} units of labor to firms $i = 1, 2$, total labor supply is $N_t = N_{1t} + N_{2t}$, the nominal wage rate the family gets is W_t, and the family uses the nominal price P_t to buy C_t units of final products from firms who produce final goods. We do not consider government taxes or transfer payment. The budget constraints the representative households face are

$$P_tC_t + Q_tB_{t+1} \leq B_t + W_tN_t. \quad (8)$$

The first-order conditions for households' optimization problems are

$$C_t^{\sigma}N_t^{\gamma} = \frac{W_t}{P_t}. \quad (9)$$

$$Q_t = \beta E_t\left\{\left(\frac{C_t}{C_{t+1}}\right)^{\sigma}\left(\frac{P_t}{P_{t+1}}\right)\right\}. \quad (10)$$

where (9) is the contemporary substitute conditions on consumption and labor; (10) is the Euler equation of consumption. The transversality condition for the optimization problem is $\lim_{t\to\infty} \beta^t B_{t+1}/P_{t+1} = 0$.

2. Representative firms

(1) Physical products firms

Assume there is a series of competitive physical products firms whose behaviors are the same in the economy; the specific form of the production function is

$$Y_{1t} = A_{1t}N_{1t}^{1-\alpha_1}, 0 < \alpha_1 < 1. \quad (11)$$

where Y_{1t} is the output level, N_{1t} is the labor input, A_{1t} represents the use of technology, and $1-\alpha_1$ represents the output elasticity of labor. In the condition of perfect competition, the price is given; the first-order condition to maximize the firm's profits is

$$\frac{W_{1t}}{P_{1t}} = (1-\alpha_1)\frac{Y_{1t}}{N_{1t}}. \quad (12)$$

W_{1t} is the nominal wage level.

(2) Services firms

Assume that services firms have the same form of production function as do products firms, that is

$$Y_{2t} = A_{2t}N_{2t}^{1-\alpha_2}, 0 < \alpha_2 < 1. \quad (13)$$

where Y_{2t} is the output level, N_{2t} is the labor input, A_{2t} represents the use of technology, and $1-\alpha_2$ represents the output elasticity of labor. In the condition of perfect competition, the price is given; the first-order condition to maximize the firm's profits is

$$\text{Max}\, \pi_{2t} = P_{2t}Y_{2t} - W_{2t}N_{2t} - \Phi(P_{2t})Y_{2t} \quad (14)$$

where W_{2t} is the nominal wage level for the services sector. $\Phi(P_{2t})$ is the price adjustment costs, following the twice concave function setting $1 > \phi'(\cdot) > 0$, $\phi''(\cdot) < 0$. In equilibrium, for a services product, the supply is equal to demand, that is $Y_{2t} = C_{2t}$,

Thus, the first-order conditions for services firms are

$$\frac{\partial \pi_{2t}}{\partial N_{2t}} = 0 \rightarrow [P_{2t} - \Phi(P_{2t})](1 - \alpha_2)A_{2t}N_{2t}^{-\alpha_2} = W_{2t} \tag{15}$$

$$\frac{\partial \pi_{2t}}{\partial P_{2t}} = 0 \rightarrow [1 - \Phi'(P_{2t})]Y_{2t} + [P_{2t} - \Phi(P_{2t})]\frac{\partial Y_{2t}}{\partial P_{2t}} = 0 \tag{16}$$

We can easily obtain $\frac{\partial Y_{2t}}{\partial P_{2t}} = (1 - \theta)(-\varepsilon)\left(\frac{P_{2t}}{P_t}\right)^{-1-\varepsilon}\left(\frac{C_t}{P_t}\right) = (-\varepsilon)\left(\frac{Y_{2t}}{P_{2t}}\right)$

Plugging it into Eq. (16):

$$1 - \Phi'(P_{2t}) = \varepsilon\left[1 - \frac{\Phi(P_{2t})}{P_{2t}}\right] \tag{17}$$

Combining(15) with (17), we can obtain

$$\frac{1 - \Phi'(P_{2t})}{\varepsilon}(1 - \alpha_2)A_{2t}N_{2t}^{-\alpha_2} = \frac{W_{2t}}{P_{2t}} \tag{18}$$

3. Equilibrium analysis

Assuming that the two products markets are clear, we can obtain $Y_{1t} = C_{1t}$, $Y_{2t} = C_{2t}$,

The total resource constraint is $Y_t = C_t$. Rearranging Eqs. (6), (11), and (13),we obtain

$$\frac{A_{1t}}{A_{2t}}\left(\frac{N_{1t}^{1-\alpha_1}}{N_{2t}^{1-\alpha_2}}\right) = \frac{\theta}{1-\theta}\left(\frac{P_{1t}}{P_{2t}}\right)^{-\varepsilon} \tag{19}$$

Assuming that labor can flow freely; we can obtain $W_{1t} = W_{2t} = W_t$. Rearranging Eqs. (12) and (18), we can obtain

$$\frac{1 - \Phi'(P_{2t})}{\varepsilon}(1 - \alpha_2)A_{2t}N_{2t}^{-\alpha_2}P_{2t} = (1 - \alpha_1)A_{1t}N_{1t}^{-\alpha_1}P_{1t} \tag{20}$$

Combining (19) with (20), we can obtain

$$\frac{N_{1t}^{(1-\alpha_1)\frac{1}{\varepsilon}+\alpha_1}}{N_{2t}^{(1-\alpha_2)\frac{1}{\varepsilon}+\alpha_2}} = \frac{\varepsilon}{1-\Phi'(\mathrm{P}_{2t})} \frac{1-\alpha_1}{1-\alpha_2} \left(\frac{\theta}{1-\theta}\right)^{\frac{1}{\varepsilon}} \left(\frac{A_{1t}}{A_{2t}}\right)^{1-\frac{1}{\varepsilon}} \tag{21}$$

For ease of analysis, assuming that, in the steady state, two sectors have the same exogenous technology, and the total CES elasticity of the two kinds of products is 1, thus

$$A_1 = A_2,\ \varepsilon = 1.$$

In the steady state, the ratio of the labor force absorbed by the two sectors is

$$\frac{N_1}{N_2} = \frac{1}{1-\Phi'(\mathrm{P}_2)} \frac{\theta}{1-\theta} \frac{1-\alpha_1}{1-\alpha_2} \tag{22}$$

We know that, in the steady state, the ratio of the labor force depends on representative households' consumption weight, the labor productivity of the two departments and price adjustment costs in the services sector. Because the model considers only labor, it shows that, in the steady state, the output ratio in the two departments also depends on these three elements. We can easily see that, in the steady state, when the physical consumption weight is larger for representative households, the efficiency of elements production is higher in the physical sector, and price adjustment costs are higher in the services sector. This will lead to a greater output of physical products and smaller outputs of services products.

Further, it can be concluded that, when the consumer's consumption structure leans to the services products (when $\boldsymbol{\theta}$ becomes smaller), the reverse changes in price adjustment costs and element production efficiency in services product firms may hinder the effect of the optimal allocation of resources when the consumption structure upgrades from physical consumption to service consumption, creating distortion in the consumption demand structure and supply structure and lowering the efficiency of factor allocation.

By contrast, suppose that institutional reform and monopoly-breaking keep services product firms and physical product firms in perfect competition. Keeping other assumptions constant and repeating the above derivation steps, we obtain the optimal labor ratio of the two types of firm in the steady-state, as follows:

$$\left(\frac{N_1}{N_2}\right)^* = \frac{\theta}{1-\theta} \frac{1-\alpha_1}{1-\alpha_2} \tag{23}$$

Compared with Eq. (22), we find that, in the two departments, the labor force ratio under the assumption of perfect competition is less than that under the assumption of monopoly, which can be expressed as follows:

$$\left(\frac{N_1}{N_2}\right)^* < \frac{N_1}{N_2} \tag{24}$$

This indicates that, after breaking the monopoly in the services sector, output in the sector will increase, and the supply structure in both the physical product and services sectors will change along with the change in the representative household's consumption structure.

Further, we assume that the CES elasticity of total products does not equal 1 and do not take into account the elements' differences in productivity (i.e., $\varepsilon \neq 1$ and $\alpha_1 = \alpha_2 = \alpha$). Subtracting the optimal labor ratios under the two assumptions about the competitive firms, we can obtain

$$D_s = \frac{N_1}{N_2} - \left(\frac{N_1}{N_2}\right)^* = \left[\frac{\varepsilon}{1-\Phi'(\mathrm{P}_2)}\left(\frac{\theta}{1-\theta}\right)^{\frac{1}{\varepsilon}}\right]^{\frac{1}{(1-\alpha)\frac{1}{\varepsilon}+\alpha}} - \frac{\theta}{1-\theta} \tag{25}$$

For the above equation, taking the partial derivative with respect to θ, we can obtain

$$\frac{\partial D_s}{\partial \theta} = \left\{\left[\frac{\varepsilon}{1-\Phi'(\mathrm{P}_2)}\right]^{\frac{1}{(1-\alpha)\frac{1}{\varepsilon}+\alpha}} \frac{1}{1+(\varepsilon-1)\alpha}\left(\frac{1-\theta}{\theta}\right)^{\frac{(\varepsilon-1)\alpha}{1+(\varepsilon-1)\alpha}} - 1\right\}\left\{\frac{1}{(1-\theta)^2}\right\}$$

If $\varepsilon > 1$ in above formula, $\left[\frac{\varepsilon}{1-\Phi'(\mathrm{P}_2)}\right]^{\frac{1}{(1-\alpha)\frac{1}{\varepsilon}+\alpha}>1}$, $\frac{1}{1+(\varepsilon-1)\alpha} < 1$, θ will effect whether $\frac{\partial D_s}{\partial \theta}$ is larger than 0 or smaller than 0. We can judge that, when $\theta < 1/2$, it is highly possible that $\frac{\partial D_s}{\partial \theta} > 0$, indicating that, when the products in the services sector are more important for representative households, the production structure leans more on physical products, the distortion of the potential resource configuration will be greater, and the supply efficiency of output will be lower.